Christian History Made Easy

Participant Guide

Timothy Paul Jones, PhD

Developed with Gabriel Etzel and Rebekah Mason

This Participant Guide accompanies the

Christian History Made Easy 12-session DVD-based study
(ISBN 9781596365254 or ISBN 9781596365261)

and

Christian History Made Easy Leader Guide
(ISBN 9781596365278)

Christian History Made Easy: Participant Guide
© 2012 Bristol Works, Inc.
Rose Publishing, LLC
P.O. Box 3473
Peabody, Massachusetts 01961-3473 USA
www.hendricksonrose.com

Scripture taken from the New American Standard Bible, ©Copyright 1960, 1962, 1963, 1968, 1971, 1972, 1973, 1975, 1977, 1995 by the Lockman Foundation. Used by permission.

Author Timothy Paul Jones is represented by Nappaland Literary Agency www.nappaland.com.

Printed in the United States of America

February 2019, 17th printing

Contents

About This Study

"We have," the author of Hebrews remarked, "so great a cloud of witnesses surrounding us" (Heb. 12:1). The Apostles' Creed echoes, "I believe ... in the communion of the saints."

What these ancient words seem to suggest is that when Christians gather, it isn't only the living that are present. In some way that transcends human understanding, the saints of the past are present too. Their presence around us points us toward Jesus Christ, "the author and perfecter of our faith" (Heb. 12:2). This cloud has grown far fuller since the first century AD, as millions who have embraced the gospel have faced death and found themselves "at home with the Lord" (2 Cor. 5:8). Together, these many men and women form the history of Christianity—a vast and beautiful story that is, if you are a Christian, your story too!

Yet many Christians find it difficult to make sense of this story. The history of Christianity can seem overwhelming, confusing, even boring—but, in truth, this story is far from boring! The history of Christianity is the story of reformers and revivalists, martyrs and crusaders. It's the true story of how the good news of Jesus has spread around the globe. It's the story of God's Spirit working through ordinary people in extraordinary ways. This story enables God's people to read their Bibles better, to evaluate their beliefs more wisely, and to understand why other Christians do what they do. The purpose of this study is to introduce you to this exciting story in a way that anyone can understand and enjoy.

Meet the Author

Dr. Timothy Paul Jones

Timothy Paul Jones is a bestselling and award-winning author, scholar, and professor of leadership at The Southern Baptist Theological Seminary. He has earned the Bachelor of Arts degree in biblical studies and pastoral ministry, the Master of Divinity with focus in history and New Testament, as well as the Doctor of Philosophy.

Dr. Jones has authored, coauthored, or contributed to more than a dozen books. He has also written numerous articles for popular ministry magazines and academic journals including *Discipleship Journal, Religious Education Journal, Christian Education Journal,* and *Perspectives in Religious Studies.* Dr. Jones has contributed to two highly-regarded reference works, *Nelson's Dictionary of Christianity* and *Nelson's New Christian Dictionary.* He has been the recipient of the Baker Book House Award, the North American Professors of Christian Education Scholastic Recognition Award, and the 2009 Retailers' Choice Award from *Christian Retailing* magazine.

Despite his strong academic pedigree, Dr. Jones has shown a unique ability to communicate in an appealing, accessible style through books such as the award-winning *Christian History Made Easy* and the best selling *The Da Vinci Codebreaker* (coauthored with James Garlow). Dr. Jones has been featured on Fox News and WGN, commenting on religious trends and topics. He is represented by Nappaland Literary Agency (www.nappaland.com) and blogs at www.timothypauljones.com.

Dr. Jones resides in Louisville, Kentucky, with his wife Rayann and daughters Hannah and Skylar. Over the past two decades, he has had the privilege of serving as a pastor in several churches. In these contexts, he saw how learning about theology and church history could help Christians to flesh out their faith in amazing ways.

Participant Guide developed with Gabriel Etzel and Rebekah Mason

Gabriel Etzel is the Associate Dean for the School of Religion at Liberty University, Lynchburg, Virginia. He holds a Doctor of Ministry degree from Liberty Baptist Theological Seminary, and is a PhD candidate at The Southern Baptist Theological Seminary. Gabe and his wife Whitney have three children, Landon, Ava, and Isaac.

Rebekah Mason is a faculty member at Silverdale Baptist Academy in Chattanooga, Tennessee, where she teaches Bible and Church History. She earned the Master of Divinity in Women's Studies and Advanced Biblical Languages from Southeastern Baptist Theological Seminary and is a candidate for the Doctor of Education at the Southern Baptist Theological Seminary.

Get the Complete DVD-Based Kit

The Kit (ISBN 9781596365254) includes everything you need to teach *Christian History Made Easy* using professionally produced video sessions, leader and participant guides, and a PowerPoint® presentation.

The Kit includes:

- DVD with 12 video sessions

- One printed *Christian History Made Easy* participant guide (ISBN 9781596365285)

- One printed copy of the award-winning full-color *Christian History Made Easy* leader guide (ISBN 9781596365278) + PDF leader guide

- One printed copy of the award-winning, full-color *Christian History Made Easy* handbook (ISBN 9781596363281)

- *Christian History Made Easy* PowerPoint® presentation on CD-ROM (ISBN 9781596363410)

- PDF files for posters, fliers, handouts, and bulletin inserts for promotion

Available at www.hendricksonrose.com or by calling
Rose Publishing at 1-800-358-3111. Also available
wherever good Christian books are sold.

SESSION 1

The First Christians

AD *1–100*

Why on earth does history matter, anyway? History matters because it's the story of how God works among his people in his world!

In the first century AD, two specific historical events—a fire in Rome and the fall of Jerusalem—caused Christians to be seen as a separate and dangerous sect. Roman governors and emperors mocked Christians, threw them to the beasts, and burned them at the stake. Yet, no matter what anyone did, God remained present among his people, working at every turn to cause the gospel to spread through the testimony of the church.

Session 1 Outline

1. History Matters Because:

   a. The gospel matters. The gospel is rooted in historical events.

   b. God's Word matters. The better we understand history, the better we can apply God's Word.

   c. God's work matters. History reminds us that God's work includes more than our own generation.

2. What Happened after Acts 28?

   a. Persecution after the fire in Rome, AD 64 (Nero)

   b. Division after the fall of Jerusalem, AD 70 (Vespasian, Titus); Christians fled Jerusalem.

   c. Deification of emperors in their lifetimes, AD 81–96 (Domitian); Christians refused to worship the emperor.

   d. Deepening persecution of Christians; Ignatius, Polycarp, and Blandina martyred.

Roman Emperors

Emperor	Reign	Description	Death
Nero	AD 54–68	The first part of his reign was peaceful, but in the second part he ordered the deaths of his chief advisors, many wealthy nobles, and even his own mother. When a massive fire in Rome struck in AD 64, he avoided culpability by blaming the Christians for it and ruthlessly persecuting them. Paul and Peter are believed to have been martyred during Nero's persecution.	Committed suicide
Vespasian	AD 69–79	Ruler after Nero who was instrumental in quelling a Jewish uprising in Jerusalem and eventually ordering his son Titus to destroy Jerusalem and the temple.	Died of illness
Titus	AD 79–81	One of Vespasian's sons, who as a military leader before becoming emperor, destroyed the temple in Jerusalem in AD 70.	Died of illness
Domitian	AD 81–96	Vespasian's youngest son, he is known for being the first emperor to demand the title "lord and god" of himself. (Traditionally, emperors were deified after their death.) He severely persecuted Christians in the later part of his reign.	Assassinated

Relief on the Arch of Titus showing Roman soldiers carrying off temple treasures after Titus' destruction of the temple in Jerusalem.

Know More About...

The first question often asked about church history is, "What's the point?" In other words, why does it matter? One historian responds to this question in this way: "Christianity is not an ethereal, eternal doctrine about God's nature, but rather it is the presence of God in the world in the person of Jesus Christ. Christianity is incarnation, and, therefore, it exists in the concrete and the historical" (Justo L. Gonzalez, *A History of Christian Thought*).

The First Christians

In the first few decades of the Christian faith, followers of Jesus struggled to help people around them understand what it really meant to be a Christian. The first Christians were Jewish, and were viewed by the Roman Empire as members of a sect of the Jewish religion. They continued to worship in the temple and practice Jewish feasts and customs. They saw faith in Jesus as the fulfillment of the hopes and dreams of Israel. Peter explained this in early sermons found in Acts 2:14–36 and Acts 3:17–25. Read these passages carefully, considering how early Christians explained their faith to the people around them in the first century.

Explaining the Christian faith is important today as well. How would you explain what it means to be a Christian to someone unfamiliar with Christianity?

_____

_____

_____

_____

_____

_____

Nero's Persecution of Christians

Following the tide of popular opinion, Roman Emperor Nero deepened negative perceptions of Christians by recognizing them as a religion separate from Judaism, then by initiating the first official persecution of Christians.

On the night of his arrest, Jesus prophesied such persecution: "Remember the word that I said to you:

Roman Emperor Nero, reigned AD 54–68

'A servant is not greater than his master.' If they persecuted me, they will also persecute you. If they kept my word, they will also keep yours. But all these things they will do to you on account of my name, because they do not know him who sent me" (John 15:20–21).

How did the first followers of Jesus respond to persecution?

_____

_____

_____

_____

_____

_____

_____

The Martyrdom of Polycarp

Polycarp the bishop of Smyrna was hunted, captured, and killed because of his faithful witness to Jesus. After being captured by the Roman authorities, Polycarp instructed his disciples to feed the soldiers that had come to arrest him while he spent an hour in prayer. After such a show of hospitality and hearing his words of faithful prayer, it is said that "his guards repented that they had been instrumental in taking him" (Foxe's Book of Martyrs). Polycarp rested in the righteousness of God, even when he was being treated unjustly. Some of Polycarp's final words were, "Eighty-six years, I have served Christ, and he has done me no wrong. How can I blaspheme my king, the one who has saved me?"

How can you provide a clear witness to the gospel, even when you are being treated unfairly or even persecuted?

_____

_____

_____

_____

_____

_____

_____

Words from the Ones Who Were There

The Apostle Peter

Peter was martyred during the reign of Nero. Peter had this to say about the suffering and persecution faced by the followers of Christ during this first wave of persecution:

"Beloved, do not be surprised at the fiery trial when it comes upon you to test you, as though something strange were happening to you. But rejoice insofar as you share Christ's sufferings, that you may also rejoice and be glad when his glory is revealed. If you are insulted for the name of Christ, you are blessed, because the Spirit of glory and of God rests upon you... Yet if anyone suffers as a Christian, let him not be ashamed, but let him glorify God in that name" (1 Peter 4:12–14, 16).

According to tradition, the apostle Peter was crucified upside-down, saying he was not worthy to be crucified in the same manner as his Lord Jesus.

Throughout the centuries that followed Peter's writing of these words, many believers faithfully followed the words and example of Peter and suffered and died for their faith.

How does Peter instruct believers to respond to trials experienced because of their faith?

_____

_____

_____

_____

_____

_____

_____

_____

First-Century Pagan Writers

The practices of the early church were often shrouded in mystery because some portions of their services were not open to those who were not Christians. The reason why unbelievers could not witness the Lord's Supper (Communion) and baptism was because early Christians saw baptism and the Lord's Supper as special ordinances. They did not want to risk any unbeliever partaking in these ordinances or trying to imitate these ordinances in a pagan context. There were frequent misunderstandings concerning their practices and beliefs. An anonymous pagan writer who obviously misconstrued the Lord's Supper imagined what the Christians might be doing during this ordinance:

"An infant is covered with dough, to deceive the innocent. The infant is placed before the person who is to be stained with their rites. The young pupil slays the infant. Thirstily, they lick up the blood! Eagerly they tear apart its limbs. After much feasting, they extinguish [the lights]. Then, the connections of depraved lusts involve them in an uncertain fate" (Quoted by Minucius Felix, Octavius 9).

Even today there are beliefs and practices of Christians that are misunderstood by the world. What are some misunderstood teachings or practices?

_____

_____

_____

_____

Read John 15:18–25. What does Jesus have to say about hatred and persecution from the world toward Christians? Summarize Jesus' teaching in the space below.

_____

_____

_____

_____

_____

Tertullian

Believers who defended their faith against rumors and misunderstandings were known as apologists. One first-century apologist, Tertullian, made this statement concerning those who viciously and ignorantly attacked Christians:

"So we maintain that they are both ignorant while they hate us, and hate us unrighteously while they continue in ignorance.... The proof of their ignorance, at once condemning and excusing their injustice, is this, that those who once hated Christianity because they knew nothing about it, no sooner come to know it than they all lay down at once their enmity. From being its haters they become its disciples. By simply getting acquainted with it, they begin now to hate what they had formerly been, and to profess what they had formerly hated" (Tertullian, *Apology*).

Tertullian argues that ignorance and fear lead to hate, but knowledge and understanding lead to faith. How can Christians today best help people who despise the gospel to understand the gospel?

_____

_____

_____

_____

_____

Family Time

Get Together: Think of people who are accused or persecuted unfairly in your family's favorite films. List as many examples as you can.

Read Together: James 1:2–4 and 1 Peter 1:6–9. How does God use unfair persecutions and false accusations to bring glory to himself?

Learn Together: John Foxe wrote of Christianity that "the history of the church may almost be said to be a history of the trials and sufferings of its members, as experienced at the hands of wicked men" (*Foxe's Book of Martyrs*). While the stories of the early Christians and martyrs are horrific, the words and actions of those believers are often full of grace, joy, strength, and forgiveness. Discuss together what you would hope to say as a testimony to the gospel if you were facing persecution for your faith.

Pray Together: "Heavenly Father, thank you for the testimony of your faithfulness to your children that we see in the lives of early Christians. Even in the face of persecution, you strengthen our faith through Jesus Christ and bring glory to yourself. Cause us by your Spirit to rest in your joy when we face trials, so that your kingdom multiplies on the earth. Amen."

SESSION 2
Defending the Truth
AD *100–300*

Roman persecutions dogged God's people from the outside! False teachings hounded the church from within! Faced with such challenging circumstances, Christians faced several crucial questions: Which writings should be seen as authoritative? Was Jesus really fully God and fully man? What does it mean to be a Christian?

These were not heady debates, limited to a few Bible colleges and theological seminaries. These were deeply practical struggles in local churches to maintain the truth of Jesus at a time when proclaiming the gospel could cost Christians their lives.

Session 2 Outline

1. Orthodoxy and Heresy

    a. Walter Bauer's hypothesis

2. Four False Perspectives on Jesus:

    a. Ebionites ("poor ones")

    b. Docetists ("I seem")

    c. Gnostics ("in the know")

    d. Marcionism

3. Three Ways that Christians Responded

a. Canon of Scripture

    i. Can the text be traced to an eyewitness or a close associate of an eyewitness?

    ii. Do other congregations accept this text as a testimony that can be traced to an eyewitness or a close associate of an eyewitness?

    iii. Does this text agree with other texts that can be traced without any doubt to an eyewitness or a close associate of an eyewitness?

b. Confession of Faith

    i. A series of questions asked at baptism that later developed into the Apostles' Creed.

c. Centralized Authority

    i. Overseers (bishops) oversaw multiple congregations and traced their teachings back to the apostles.

Key Terms

Apostles' Creed – Early Christian confession of faith. This confession was not written by the apostles. The name "Apostles' Creed" means that the creed contains the truths that the apostles taught. Though the date the creed was written remains unknown, similar statements in the creed can be found in the second-century AD "Rule of Faith."

Bishop – Church leader responsible for looking after a church's faithfulness. Interchangeable with "elder" or "pastor" among early Christians (Acts 20:17–28; 1 Peter 5:1–3).

Canon – (*kanon*, "measuring stick") Group of writings that God inspired to tell the story of Jesus and to mark out the boundaries of Christian beliefs.

Docetism – (*dokeo*, "to seem") Heresy that claimed that Jesus only seemed to possess a physical body.

Ebionism – (*ebyonim*, "poor ones") Heresy that claimed that Jesus was a human Messiah, but not divine, and that God adopted Jesus at his baptism.

Gnosticism – (*gnostikos*, "knowing") Heresy that claimed that the creator of the physical world was evil, and only secret knowledge can reconnect people with the supreme deity.

"Gospel of Peter" – An early second-century AD writing that was rejected as an authoritative account of Jesus' life because it could not be clearly connected to the apostle Peter and because some passages in the book could be misconstrued to suggest that Jesus wasn't fully human. Perhaps partially preserved in Codex Papyrus Cairo 10759.

Gospel – (*godspel*, "good message") The life, death, and resurrection of Jesus by which God establishes his kingdom in the world and makes sinners right with himself through faith.

Heresy – (*hairesis*, "choosing a sect") A teaching that contradicts the essential truths about Jesus as believed and proclaimed by the apostles.

Inerrancy – Belief that the inspired human authors of the Scriptures never affirmed anything contrary to fact when writing the texts that became part of the biblical canon. As a result, Christians can be confident that the Bible never errs.

Marcionism – (from Marcion of Sinope, an early leader) Heresy that claimed that the God of the Old Testament and the God of the New Testament were two different deities.

Muratorian Fragment – Possibly the oldest list of the books included in the New Testament canon, dating to the mid-second century AD. It lists all four Gospels, Acts, and Paul's 13 epistles.

Orthodox – (*orthos* [straight] + *doxa* [opinion, expectation]) The essential truths about Jesus that were proclaimed by the apostles and preserved by early Christians.

Shepherd of Hermas – Popular second-century AD Christian writing. Some Christians thought it should be read alongside the books that would later be recognized as the New Testament. The Muratorian Fragment reveals why this text was not recognized as an authoritative text for Christians: "Hermas composed *Shepherd* quite recently—in our own times, in the city of Rome. ... So while it should indeed be read, it ought not to be read publicly for the people of the church—it is counted neither among the [Old Testament] prophets (for their number has been completed) nor among the apostles (for it is after their time)."

Christ as the Good Shepherd, third century fresco in the San Callisto Catacomb (underground burial chamber) in Rome. Catacombs were used by early Christians for burying martyrs and for hiding during times of persecution.

Know More About...

Gnosticism

Gnosticism was a belief system that adapted to various religions over the centuries. Even Judaism was affected by the Gnostic teaching that secret knowledge brings salvation. Gnosticism never stood on its own as a religion. Instead, Gnostic teachers took existing ideas and used them in twisted ways. When attached to Christianity, "Gnostic teachers often claimed that the apostles [of Jesus] had secretly revealed their teachings to a few close followers. Without this secret knowledge, humans cannot be saved" (David W. Bercot, *A Dictionary of Early Christian Beliefs*).

Do you know any examples of cults or other religious groups today that claim to have some secret teaching that brings salvation? Or perhaps a group that claims their leader received a special, authoritative revelation beyond what God revealed through Jesus?

Ebionism

The ancient Ebionites believed that Jesus was the Messiah promised to the nation of Israel in the Old Testament. The problem was, they also taught that Jesus was a mere human being called by God, not God in human flesh.

According to the writings of church leaders such as Irenaeus and Tertullian, Ebionites used only the Gospel of Matthew, rejected the teachings of Paul, and treated observance of the Jewish law as necessary to be made right with God.

In his letter to the Galatians, the apostle Paul addressed the false teaching of some who taught that believers must follow the Old Testament laws in order to be right with God. Paul wrote to the churches in Galatia, "It was for freedom that Christ set us free; therefore keep standing firm and do not be subject again to a yoke of slavery. Behold I, Paul, say to you that if you receive circumcision, Christ will be of no benefit to you.... For in Christ Jesus neither circumcision nor uncircumcision means anything, but faith working through love" (Gal. 5:1–2, 6).

Why does relying on keeping certain laws—or any regulation or ritual—to be made right with God cause Jesus to be "of no benefit to you"?

_____

_____

_____

_____

John 1:1–18, John 20:26–30, and Philippians 2:5–11 give powerful descriptions of the nature of Jesus. Read these passages of Scripture and briefly explain how they present Jesus as God in human flesh.

_____

_____

_____

_____

_____

_____

The Canon

False teaching has been a problem for the church from the very beginning. In the Gospels, we read that those who opposed Jesus claimed he was demon-possessed or insane (John 10:19–21); Paul wrote to pastors and churches, warning them of the dangers of those who added to or took away from the gospel (1 Tim. 6:3–5).

One way that the early church curtailed false teachings was by relying on texts that came from eyewitnesses of the risen Jesus or close associates of these eyewitnesses. The results of this process are known as the canon, from the Greek word for a measuring stick. The twenty-seven books of the New Testament comprise the Christian canon.

The earliest known list of New Testament books was discovered in a Latin fragment, known as the Muratorian fragment. Named for Muratori, the man who discovered the fragment in 1740, the list is a translation of a second-century Greek manuscript.

Suppose that a close friend becomes convinced that certain "lost Gospels" such as Gospel of Judas and Gospel of Thomas represent truth about Jesus that the church suppressed. How would you explain how the twenty-seven texts in the New Testament canon were selected? How could you help your friend to understand that these texts represent true, eyewitness testimony about Jesus?

_____

_____

_____

_____

Words from the Ones Who Were There

Apostle John and Polycarp

The apostle John

Polycarp, the leading pastor of Smyrna in the second century, quoted his teacher the apostle John as saying, "Whoever does not confess that Jesus Christ has come in the flesh is antichrist." Polycarp goes on to write, "Whoever does not confess the testimony of the cross is of the devil; and whosoever perverts the sayings of the Lord to suit his own lusts and says there is neither resurrection or judgment—such a one is the first-born of Satan. Let us, therefore, forsake the vanity of the crowd and false teachings and turn back to the word delivered to us from the beginning" (Polycarp, *Letter to the Philippians* 7:1–2).

Polycarp had harsh words for those who denied the essentials of the gospel message, calling them "antichrist" and "first-born of Satan." Why was Polycarp so passionate about preserving the basic teachings about the Jesus and the gospel at this particular point in church history?

_____

_____

_____

_____

What if Polycarp wrote an intense letter like this to your church. How would your church respond? How would you?

_____

_____

_____

_____

Hippolytus

Hippolytus, a third-century theologian, wrote, "The Ebionites ... say that Jesus was justified by fulfilling the Law. They also say that it was because of this that He was called Jesus and the Christ of God, for no one else had observed the Law completely.... In short, they assert that our Lord Himself was a man in a like sense with all of us" (Hippolytus. c. 225, 5.114).

In what ways are the teachings of the Ebionites similar to the teachings of certain religious groups today?

_____

_____

_____

_____

The Muratorian Fragment

The inclusion of the four Gospels—Matthew, Mark, Luke, and John—is explained in the following quote from the Muratorian Fragment: "Although different matters are taught us in the various books of the Gospels, there is no difference as regards the faith of believers. For in all of them, everything was related under one imperial Spirit."

Who or what unifies the four Gospels of the New Testament—and, in fact, all of the books of the Bible? (See 1 Peter 1:20–21 and 2 Tim. 3:16–17).

_____

_____

_____

_____

How would you explain to an unbeliever why there are four different Gospels in the New Testament?

_____

_____

_____

_____

_____

_____

Family Time

Get Together: The Christian canon refers to all the books in the New Testament as well as the Jewish Scriptures that we know as the Old Testament. However the word canon can also mean a list of essential, high-quality works. Just for fun, make a "canon" of writings for your family. What books are essential reading in your family at certain times in your life? What makes these books so important to your family? What would your family miss if these books suddenly no longer existed?

Read Together: Revelation 22:18–19

Learn Together: This passage in Revelation referred only to the book of Revelation, but it reveals how passionate early Christians were about protecting the texts that came from eyewitnesses of Jesus. When Marcion removed portions of the New Testament that he did not like, early Christians removed Marcion from leadership in the church.

How should we in our family respond to Scripture texts that we do not agree with?

Pray Together: "Father, thank you for the gift of your Word to us! Cause us to know and to understand your Word so that we can become more like Jesus. Work in us by your Spirit to convict us and to transform us for your glory. Amen."

SESSION 3

Persecuted to Preferred

AD *300–500*

After decades of experiencing vicious persecution, Christianity suddenly became the preferred religion of the Roman Empire! The story goes that Emperor Constantine saw a vision in the sky, chalked a Christian symbol on his soldiers' shields, then began crediting the God of the Christians for his military victories. Constantine actively promoted Christianity and even convened the first church-wide council in which Christian leaders from across the empire met at Nicaea to deal with heresies—but these changes came at a cost. When it came to maintaining the purity of the gospel, imperial favor wasn't always as favorable as it had seemed at first.

Session 3 Outline

1. How Roman Persecution of Christians Ended

   a. Emperor Diocletian planned for peace by splitting the empire into East and West (AD 286).

   b. On his deathbed, Emperor Galerius decreed that the persecution of Christians should end (AD 311).

   c. Constantine conquered Rome with a Christian symbol on his soldiers' shields (AD 312) and his Edict of Milan legalized Christianity (AD 313).

2. The Problem with Arius

   a. Arius taught that Jesus was a lesser being than God the Father.

   b. Council of Nicaea rejected Arius' teachings (AD 325).

   c. Athanasius stood up to Emperor Constantine when Constantine wanted to allow Arius back in the church.

Key Terms

Arianism – (from Arius, founder of the movement) Heretical belief that Jesus was created and that his divinity was not equal to God the Father.

Chi-Rho – In the fourth century, Emperor Constantine popularized the Chi-Rho symbol. It is a Christian symbol made from two Greek letters, Chi (X) and Rho (P), which are the first two letters of "Christ" in Greek (ΧΡΙΣΤΟΣ or *Christos*). These two letters were also the first two letters of a common name that meant "useful" (ΧΡΗΣΤΟΣ or *Chrestos*). Constantine may have used the Chi-Rho because it had a double meaning that Christians saw as an expression of their faith, while others would simply see it as a reference to strength or usefulness.

Council of Nicaea (AD 325) – First ecumenical (church-wide) council called by Emperor Constantine in the city of Nicaea (in modern-day Turkey) to deal with the teachings of an elder named Arius. The council overwhelmingly denounced Arianism and formulated the Creed of Nicaea.

Edict of Milan (AD 313) – Letter signed by emperors Constantine and Licinius that legalized all religions in the Roman Empire, including Christianity. This effectively ended Christian persecution by emperors.

Heresy – (from *hairesis*, "choosing a sect") A teaching that contradicts the essential truths about Jesus as believed and proclaimed by the apostles.

Monk – (from *monakhos*, "alone") In the fourth century, a man who isolated himself in the deserts to diminish temptations and to become closer to God.

Orthodox – (*orthos* [straight] + *doxa* [opinion, expectation]) The essential truths about Jesus that were proclaimed by the apostles and preserved by early Christians.

Trinity – Christian doctrine that teaches there is one God who exists eternally in three Persons: God the Father, God the Son, and God the Holy Spirit.

Chi-Rho Symbol

Know More About...

The Rapid Spread of the Gospel

The development of Christianity from a persecuted sect of Judaism to the preferred religion of the Roman Empire occurred in a relatively brief period of time. The relative stability of the Roman Empire had allowed Christians to travel freely and share their faith. God, in his sovereignty, initiated the coming of Christ to take place at a time when the gospel could spread through a land with a central government and common language.

With this rapid spread of the gospel also came rapid confusion concerning the truth of Jesus and rapid conflict with established powers. The challenges of heresy and persecution demanded that believers find unity in essential, orthodox beliefs. If people were dying for their beliefs, it was vital to know what truths they were dying for.

The Donatist Controversy

Unity within the body of Christ was a specific prayer request of Jesus (John 17:22–23). But unity hasn't always come easily among God's people!

When ancient Christians faced persecution, not everyone stood strong. In fact, some church members denied their faith to save their lives. Others obtained forged papers to protect themselves and their families. When persecution ended, some church members confessed their sin, repented, and asked to rejoin their churches.

This pattern led to some difficult questions in the churches! When church members denied Jesus to save their lives, did this mean they hadn't truly been Christians? Or were they true believers whose faithfulness had faltered in a moment of weakness? If they weren't really Christians, they shouldn't simply be accepted back into the fellowship of their churches! But if they were repentant believers, the right response was to embrace them because their righteousness depended not on their actions but on the finished work of Jesus.

A man named Donatus said it was wrong to allow those who had denied the faith to return to fellowship with believers who had endured persecution.

Cyprian, a North African overseer, claimed that this was an opportunity to show grace to repentant brothers and sisters.

Eventually, many of the churches split over this issue.

Jesus told his disciples, "A new commandment I give to you, that you love one another, even as I have loved you, that you also love one another. By this all men will know that you are My disciples, if you have love for one another" (John 13:34–35).

How do you think you might have responded to your fellow believers if you had lived during the Donatist controversy? How can Christians today work through difficult and complicated questions while still obeying the command of Jesus to love one another?

_____

_____

_____

_____

Give an example of a situation in which it may be necessary to agree to disagree. Then, give an example of a situation in which it is necessary to stand firm in your beliefs and behaviors.

_____

_____

_____

_____

The Council of Nicaea

Arius, an elder in Alexandria, taught that Jesus was not God! Instead, Jesus was God's first creation. Many church leaders strongly opposed these false claims from Arius.

Constantine called a council of church leaders to prevent division in his empire. He called the council to meet in the village of Nicaea, near his military headquarters. When the council began, Constantine proclaimed himself a church overseer and an apostle, then declared the council ready to do business.

Council of Nicaea, AD 325

The Council of Nicaea denounced Arianism, and Constantine enforced the ruling by exiling overseers who stood with Arius. Shortly afterward, it became clear that Constantine's concern was imperial unity, not doctrinal purity. Constantine commanded that Arius be brought back into the church's fellowship, even though Arius still taught that Jesus was not fully and uniquely divine.

How should believers respond when the church becomes a means to achieve political goals instead of a community that makes the gospel visible to the world?

_____

_____

_____

_____

_____

Meditate on Mark 9:38–50. Thinking about this passage in particular, how do you think that you might have responded if you were a believer in the years following the Council of Nicaea?

_____

_____

_____

_____

_____

How does this event in history affect how you think about power, politics, and the sovereignty of God?

_____

_____

_____

_____

_____

Athanasius' Determination

Athanasius, the leading pastor in Alexandria, faced opposition from Emperor Constantine and from his successor, Emperor Julian. Despite persecution, Athanasius refused to waver when it came to the orthodox teachings of the apostles about Jesus. He became known as *Athanasius Contra Mundi*: "Athanasius against the world." One historian remarked about Athanasius, "He became the symbol of the Nicene faith, and his repeated exiles and returns serve as a weather vane to show which way the doctrinal and political winds were blowing" (Justo L. Gonzalez).

Maintaining faith can be difficult in times of trial. List three Scriptures that could be particularly encouraging in hard times. Memorize these verses so that these words of truth and encouragement are with you always.

_____

_____

_____

_____

_____

Words from the Ones Who Were There

Ancient Christians

Very early in the church's history, Christians began to sing summaries of their faith, such as the *Gloria Patri*:

"Glory be to the Father and to the Son and to the Holy Ghost. As it was in the beginning, is now and ever shall be, world without end! Amen."

How do doctrinal summaries in creeds and songs help us to hold firmly to sound teachings about God and the gospel?

_____

_____

_____

_____

_____

Athanasius

"It was our sorry case that caused the Word to come down, our transgression that called out His love for us, so that He made haste to help us and to appear among us. It is we who were the cause of His taking human form, and [it was] for our salvation that in His great love He was born and manifested in a human body" (*On the Incarnation*).

Because of his great love, God came to earth in the form of a man. To have the power and authority to save, Jesus had to be fully God. To represent humanity as the perfectly-obedient sacrifice, he had to be fully man. Study Romans 3:21–31 and Hebrews chapter 2. Copy phrases below that might help you to explain to others why Jesus had to be fully God and fully man.

_____

_____

_____

_____

_____

Family Time

Get Together: Have each person write on a three-by-five card one essential belief about Jesus. Play a round of "Win, Lose, or Draw." Have each person try to draw the belief about Jesus written on his or her card. List all of the beliefs in the space below. Do you know anyone who denies one or more of these beliefs?

Read Together: Hebrews 2:14–18

Learn Together: What essential beliefs about Jesus can be found in this passage in Hebrews? Now read 2 Thessalonians 2:14–17. How can Christians today stand firm for the truth about Jesus?

In the fourth century, Athanasius stood firm for the truth about Jesus at a time when the teachings of Arius were very popular. Tell the story of Arius, the Council of Nicaea, and Athanasius. Discuss as a family how you can stand firmly for the truth about Jesus.

Pray Together: "Father God, thank you for the lives of early Christians that testify to your faithfulness from generation to generation. Son of God, guide us to grow in our knowledge of you so that we stand firm for your truth in our generation. Spirit of God, convict us when we are tempted to compromise the truth of the gospel for the sake of popularity and personal comfort. In the name of Jesus Christ our Lord, Amen."

SESSION 4
Christianity on the Move
AD *300–500*

It's one thing to live as a Christian in a world where your faith is persecuted and oppressed. Life may be hard but the boundaries between belief and unbelief are fairly clear. It's quite another to be faithful when the name "Christian" is not persecuted but praised, and even endowed with power! Some Christians responded to this new state of affairs by moving to monastic communities deep in the deserts of Egypt and North Africa. Meanwhile, barbarians from Asia and northern Europe were migrating southward into the Western Empire. As Rome was repeatedly sacked and the Western Empire fragmented, Christian leaders like Augustine helped believers to take a new perspective on the powers that surrounded them.

Session 4 Outline

1. Monks Moved to the Desert.

   a. Gregory of Nazianzus joined Basil's monastic community.

   b. Apollinaris taught that Jesus did not have a human spirit; Gregory of Nazianzus argued against this heresy.

   c. Council of Constantinople (AD 381): Jesus was recognized once again as fully God and fully man.

2. Roman Empire Fell to Barbarians.

   a. Barbarians moved south and west into the Roman Empire.

   b. Visigoth barbarians sacked Rome (AD 410).

    c.   Augustine of Hippo wrote *The City of God* to help Christians respond to the charge that Christianity caused the fall of Rome.

3.   Church Councils and Controversies Continued.

    a.   Council of Ephesus (AD 431): Jesus was one person.

    b.   Council of Chalcedon (AD 451): Jesus had two natures.

4.   Monks and Nuns Preserved Learning.

    a.   Benedict and Scholastica established monasteries that included schools.

    b.   Gregory became the first bishop of Rome from a monastic background and one of the first individuals to exercise the power that would become associated with the title "pope" (AD 590).

Key Terms

Apollinarianism – (from Apollinaris, early proponent) Heretical belief that Jesus possessed a human body, but the divine Word replaced his human mind, so that Jesus did not have a human spirit. Form of monophysitism.

Benedictine Rule – Developed by Benedict of Nursia, it provided precepts for monastic communities that included, not primarily solitude, but rhythms of rest, work, and study of Scripture. It shaped monasticism in the Middle Ages.

Catholic – (from Greek, *kath'olou*, "according to the whole") Worldwide, accepted by all; originally a reference to the beliefs and patterns embraced by all Christians throughout the world.

Dyophysitism – (from Greek, "two natures") Orthodox belief that Jesus has two natures, one human and one divine, which work in perfect harmony with one another.

Eutychianism – (after Eutyches, early proponent) Heretical belief that Jesus' divine nature absorbed his human nature to form one mixed nature. Form of monophysitism.

Great Cappadocians – Eastern Church leaders who helped fourth-century Christians clarify their beliefs about the Trinity.

Monk – (from *monakhos*, "alone") At first, a man who isolated himself in the deserts to diminish temptations and to become closer to God.

Monophysitism – (from Greek, "one nature") Heretical belief that Jesus had only one nature instead of having both a human nature and a divine nature.

Nestorianism – (after Nestorius, accused of teaching this view) Heretical belief that Jesus was two persons in one body. More properly known as hyper-dyophysitism. A popular title for the Virgin Mary was *Theotokos* meaning "bearer of God." Nestorius however preferred *Christokos* meaning "bearer of the Messiah." This controversy eventually lead to the Council of Ephesus.

Nun – (from *nonna*, Latin for an elderly tutor) A woman who joined a religious community, vowing obedience and choosing not to marry or to own property.

Pope – (from Latin for "father") At first, title for any bishop in a major city. As the Roman church's power grew in the Western Empire, it became a title reserved for the bishop of Rome.

The Vulgate – The Latin version of the Bible translated by Jerome in the fourth century AD. It became the most commonly used translation of the Bible in the Roman Catholic Church in the Middle Ages.

Church Councils in the Fourth and Fifth Centuries

Council	Year	Issue	Conclusion
Nicaea	325	Arianism	First church-wide council, produced the Creed of Nicaea; Jesus is equal to God the Father.
Constantinople	381	Apollinarianism	Second church-wide council, approved the Nicene Creed; Jesus was both human and divine.
Ephesus	431	Nestorianism	Third church-wide council, clarified that Jesus was one person, not two persons in one body.
Chalcedon	451	Eutychianism	Fourth church-wide council, clarified that, though Jesus was one person, he possessed human and divine natures.

Views of Jesus in Christian History

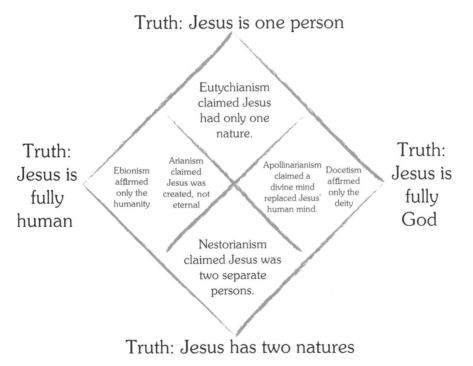

Truth: Jesus is one person

Eutychianism claimed Jesus had only one nature.

Truth: Jesus is fully human

Ebionism affirmed only the humanity

Arianism claimed Jesus was created, not eternal

Apollinarianism claimed a divine mind replaced Jesus' human mind.

Docetism affirmed only the deity

Truth: Jesus is fully God

Nestorianism claimed Jesus was two separate persons.

Truth: Jesus has two natures

The Nicene Creed

The "Symbol of the Faith" from the Council of Constantinople (AD 381), based on the Creed of Nicaea (AD 325)

"We believe in one God,
the Father Almighty,
Maker of heaven and earth,
and of all things visible and invisible."

"We believe in one Lord,
Jesus Christ the One and Only Son of God,
begotten of the Father before all ages,
light of light, very God of very God,
begotten not created,
being of the same essence with the Father;
by him all things were made;
he for us men and for our salvation came down;
he was incarnate by the Holy Spirit of the Virgin Mary;
he was made man;
he was crucified for us under Pontius Pilate;
he suffered death and was buried;
the third day he rose again according to the Scriptures,
ascended into heaven, and sits at the Father's right hand;
from there, he will return in glory to judge the living and the dead;
his kingdom will have no end."

"We believe in the Holy Spirit,
the Lord and Giver of life,
who proceeds from the Father,
who together with the Father and the Son is worshiped and glorified,
who spoke by the prophets, and in one, holy, catholic, apostolic Church;
we acknowledge one baptism unto remission of sins;
we look for the resurrection of the dead
and the life of the world to come."

Know More About...

Spiritual Leadership

Misconceptions concerning leadership are nothing new. While Jesus still walked the earth, his disciples argued amongst themselves about who was the greatest. When Jesus confronted them about their desire to rule like human lords in his kingdom, this was his challenge: "If anyone wants to be first, he shall be last of all and servant of all" (Mark 9:35).

Only when believers understand that to follow King Jesus means humbling ourselves and becoming servant-leaders can the world authentically glimpse what leadership ought to look like in God's kingdom.

Near the end of the fourth century, Christianity became the official religion of the Roman Empire. With the meshing of church and state, it became increasingly difficult to distinguish between earthly lordship and spiritual leadership. At the same time, Rome was repeatedly sacked; plagues and natural disasters took hundreds of thousands of lives. Destruction, loss, and fear led to people seeking comfort and answers, and many men and women turned to the church for both.

How would you describe the spiritual leadership that you see displayed in your home and your church?

_____

_____

_____

_____

Monks and Nuns

Throughout Scripture, people encountered God in the wilderness, in the desert, in places of exile. From Moses to the nation of Israel, from John the Baptist to Paul and even Jesus himself, the isolation and a sense of exile drove some to rely more deeply on God, even as others became more focused on themselves.

Benedict of Nursia (c. 480–543)

39

With the end of persecution and the fall of ancient empires, many Christians felt like fleeing to a place where the standards of holiness were higher and the crumbling of human kingdoms no longer mattered. These men and women became known as "monks" and "nuns."

One man, Anthony of Egypt, is credited with being one of the first to live as a hermit in the wilderness. Benedict of Nursia became one of the first to establish a set of written standards for monastic communities.

Two main motives can be observed in those who adopted the monastic life: escape and example. Many wanted to escape the distractions of the world so that they could focus on living holier lives. Yet others were looking to the examples of godly men in Scripture, like John the Baptist.

Jesus called his followers to be in the world yet not of the world (John 15:19; 17:14–16). In the boxes below, list ways that Christians should live in the world as well as ways that Christians must remain not of the world.

Circle aspects of living in the world and not of the world that would have been easier for monks and nuns. Place an X across items that would have been difficult or impossible for monks and nuns. Look carefully at both lists. What were the strengths and weaknesses of the monastic lifestyle?

In the World	Not of the World

Honoring God in Everything

Trained in rhetoric and law, John Chrysostom in the fourth century converted to Christianity as an adult and left his profession as a lawyer to become a pastor. Instead of becoming aloo servant of the state, John endured one exile at the hands of the empress of the Eastern Empire Eudoxia and died en route to a second exile.

John used his training in rhetoric and law to minister to others. Any God-honoring vocation can become a means for ministry. How can your vocation serve as a springboard to serve others in ways that testify to the power of the gospel?

_____

_____

_____

_____

_____

As overseer of Constantinople, John Chrysostom emphasized purity and righteous living among clergy and congregants. He preached messages discussing the role of parents and the church in educating young people. He encouraged more than just theological education. He understood that all of life is a theater for the glory of God.

How can you glorify God by learning more about subjects like math, science, social studies, and the arts?

_____

_____

_____

_____

_____

The Succession of Popes

Within the first century or so of Christianity, key cities had bishops or overseers that maintained orthodox teachings of the church within their regions. The rise of heresies and other conflicts increased as the number of believers increased, which led to an increase in the power and importance of these bishops. In these times of turmoil, it's easy to see why consistent and centralized leadership would have seemed like a great idea.

The bishop in Rome began to grow in influence and authority. Church tradition states that both Peter and Paul were martyred in Rome. Over time, the bishop of Rome became perceived by many church members in the Western Empire as a "pope"—as a spiritual father over all the churches. Still today, Roman Catholics see Matthew 16:18 as a recognition of Peter as the first pope receiving the "keys to the kingdom."

What is your perspective on a unique role and expanded power for the bishop of Rome?

_____

_____

_____

_____

_____

How might the political prestige that was already centered in the city of Rome have influenced the increased prestige of the bishop of Rome?

_____

_____

_____

_____

_____

Words from the Ones Who Were There

John Chrysostom

John Chrysostom looked to Proverbs 1:7 as a foundational verse for his understanding of education. He wrote the following explanation of his thoughts on education:

"Let us then implant in [the child] this wisdom and let us exercise him therein, that he may know the meaning of human desires, wealth, reputation, power, and may disdain these and strive after the highest. And let us bring words of exhortation to his mind: 'My child, fear God alone and fear none other but Him.'"

Meditate on Proverbs 1:7. What does it mean to "fear" the Lord? How does fear of the Lord make a difference in knowledge, wisdom, and instruction?

_____

_____

_____

_____

The Fall of Rome

During the third and fourth centuries, tragedy after tragedy drove people to struggle to make some sense of their world. After the fall of Rome, one ancient writer stated:

"If only to this end have the barbarians been sent within Roman borders ... that the church of Christ might be filled with Huns and Suebi, with Vandals and Burgundians, with diverse and innumerable peoples of believers, then let God's mercy be praised ... even if this has taken place through our own destruction" (Paulus Orosius, *History Against the Pagans*).

God works even through tragic events for the glory of his Son and for the good of his people (Rom. 8:28–29). Describe an event below that seemed tragic but that God used for his glory.

_____

_____

_____

_____

_____

_____

_____

Ancient Visigoth Christian church building in Spain

Family Time

Get Together: Talk about what it means to be a servant leader, in the biblical sense: giving up one's own rights and privileges for the sake of leading others toward godliness (see Phil. 2:1–11). How can each family member be both leader and servant? How can older siblings show leadership by serving younger siblings? How can parents model servant leadership to their children? From chores and housework to times of family worship, servant leadership begins in the home. Discover together ways that your family members can help one another to practice Jesus-centered servant leadership.

Read Together: Mark 8:34–38

Learn Together: Augustine of Hippo is a prime example of a church leader whose life was transformed by taking up his cross and following Jesus.

As a young man, Augustine traded the Christian faith of his mother for the pursuit of personal pleasure and prestige. But the more Augustine chased after the things that he thought would make him happy, the more God pursued him. The convicting work of the Holy Spirit within Augustine seemed to challenge every argument that Augustine presented against Christian faith. In the end, Augustine's attention became focused on a single biblical text: Romans 13:11–14. Happening upon this text, Augustine finally admitted that Jesus Christ was Lord, not only of the world but also of his life.

Augustine became a servant leader, both as a bishop of the North African church in Hippo and as a prolific writer and defender of orthodox faith. Talents and personality traits that had once led him to seek his own pleasure became the very tools God used to advance the gospel in the fourth and fifth centuries. His ability to reason, to write clearly, and to love people led to Augustine being one of the most influential servants in the history of the church.

Pray Together: "Father beyond us, thank you for showing us how you accomplish your will in this world through ordinary people and painful circumstances. Christ sent for us, increase our faith as we seek to serve you by serving one another. Spirit among us, give us boldness to guide others toward citizenship in the city of God. We love you and adore you, three-personed God. Amen."

SESSION 5

A Church Divided

AD *500–1300*

The East and West grew further apart! King and bishops grew more deeply entwined! Kings forced professions of faith, and popes called for brutal Crusades! But these Crusades, far from unifying East and West, climaxed with the shattering of Christianity into two communions, Eastern Orthodox and Roman Catholic.

Session 5 Outline

1. Icon Controversy

2. The Franks

    a. Charlemagne (Charles the Great) forced Christian conversions.

    b. Pope Leo III crowned Charlemagne as emperor (800).

    c. Alcuin of York led the Carolingian Renaissance.

3. Three Reasons Why the Church Split

    a. One word added to a creed

      i.   Western Christians added the word *filioque* ("and the Son") to the Nicene Creed; Eastern Christians objected.

b.   A bull on a communion table

      i.   The bishop of Constantinople refused to recognize Pope Leo IX; In response, the pope had an insulting papal bull laid on the communion table in the Church of Holy Wisdom in Constantinople (1054).

c.   A tragic sack of an ancient city

      i.   Pope Urban II called for a Crusade against Muslims in the Holy Land (1095).

     ii.   Peter the Hermit caused trouble in Constantinople.

    iii.   Western Crusaders sacked Constantinople in the Fourth Crusade (1204).

Key Terms

Carolingian Renaissance – Charlemagne's initiative, overseen by the monk Alcuin of York, to preserve and to spread classical learning through monasteries.

Council of Nicaea, Second (AD 787) – Seventh and last church-wide council concluded that veneration of two-dimensional icons does not violate the biblical command against graven images.

Crusades – Series of military expeditions launched by European Christians against Muslims to conquer the Holy Land. Pope Urban II called for the First Crusade in 1095. Four years later in 1099, the First Crusade conquered Jerusalem, slaughtering thousands of Jews and Muslims in the city. The Crusades lasted into the thirteenth century.

Filioque – Latin word meaning "and the Son" which Western Christians added to the Nicene Creed in the 800s, so that the creed indicated that the Holy Spirit proceeded from the Father and the Son (see John 15:26). Eastern Christians objected to this addition, citing the church's agreement not to alter the Nicene Creed as established in the Council of Ephesus four centuries earlier.

Icons – Image of a biblical character or a sacred individual in church history, created for the purpose of religious veneration.

Iconoclasts – Those who destroy icons. Iconoclasts were "icon-smashers" and saw all reverence for icons as idolatry.

Iconodules – Those who revere icons. Iconodules were "icon-kissers" and saw reverence for icons as a way of remembering and rejoicing in how God had worked through past believers.

Papal Bull – A decree issued by the bishop of Rome. "Bulla" referred to the lead seal, with the pope's name on one side and the images of Peter and Paul on the other, that popes used to prevent anyone from tampering with the decree.

Roman Catholic and Eastern Orthodox Comparison

	Roman Catholicism	Eastern Orthodoxy
Name	"Catholic" means "worldwide" or "universal."	"Orthodoxy" means "correct belief" or "correct worship" and implies faithfulness to the church's ancient teachings and traditions.
Structure	The bishop or overseer of Rome is the father ("pope") over all churches. He represents Christ's leadership in the church. Overseers ("bishops") guide each region and are responsible directly to the pope. High overseers ("archbishops") are highly esteemed by other bishops, but they have no power outside their own regions. Since 1150, bishops and archbishops who advise the pope have been known as "cardinal" overseers.	Today, the Orthodox Church consists of several self-ruling groups of churches. A metropolitan patriarch ("city father") guides each group of churches. Some patriarchs also serve as high overseers ("archbishops"). Orthodox Christians highly esteem the patriarch of Constantinople (modern Istanbul, Turkey). Yet he has little official authority beyond his own churches.
Authority	Scripture as interpreted and expounded through church councils, church tradition, and bishops in union with the pope.	The teachings of the apostles as understood through the Scriptures, the first seven church-wide councils, and the ancient church fathers.

St. Peter's Basilica at the Vatican, Rome

Eastern Orthodox Church in Ukraine

Know More About...

Being in the World, but Not of the World

From the fourth century forward, emperors became entangled in the practices and leadership of churches. In some ways, it seemed as if the health of the church became inseparably linked to the health of the empire. When the eastern and western halves of the ancient Roman Empire drifted apart, so did the churches. During the Middle Ages, this drift between the empires became a full-scale rupture among the churches. The result was that Christianity became fragmented into two communions, Eastern Orthodox and Roman Catholic.

Jesus commanded his followers to remain *in the world* yet never to become *of the world* (John 17:16–18). Sometimes, instead of being in the world but not of the world, those who claim the name of Christ become both *in the world* and *of the world*. They interact with their culture (which is good!) but they also absorb the values of their culture (that's not so good). They pursue the world's ways of gaining and exercising power. That's part of what happened in the centuries after Emperor Constantine first favored Christianity. Jesus warned against the church becoming a political power: "You know that the rulers in this world lord it over their people, and officials flaunt their authority over those under them. But among you it will be different" (Mark 10:42–43). Yet the church and the empire became so intertwined that church leaders increasingly used the empire's power to achieve the church's goals or used the empire's methods to expand their own power.

Other times, Christians try to be *neither in the world nor of the world*. That's what some people in Corinth misconstrued Paul's words to mean. When Paul heard that some were refusing even to associate with non-Christians, he responded, "I wrote to you in my letter not to associate with sexually immoral people—not at all meaning the people of this world.... In that case you would have to leave this world!" (1 Cor. 5:9–10). When Christians try to "leave this world," they lose the capacity to engage intelligently with the questions and ideas that arise in the culture around them. In some instances, this happened among monks and nuns—though many men and women in the monastic movement also served their communities and preserved the best elements of their culture as well.

What Jesus commanded his followers was to be *in the world* yet *not of the world*. This means speaking the truth of the gospel in ways that people around us can understand while refusing to embrace the world's methods or values. This wasn't easy for Jesus' first followers, it wasn't easy for churches in the Middle Ages, and it's still difficult for us today.

The Carolingian Renaissance

In the ninth century, a movement known as the Carolingian Renaissance resulted in rapid and helpful developments in education and culture. The man who provided the initial impulse for this movement was the first emperor of a renewed empire that would become known centuries later as a Holy Roman Empire. His name was Charles, but he is better known as Charles the Great or Charlemagne.

Through the leadership of Charlemagne and under the direction of a monk Alcuin of York, education and religion in Europe became standardized during what became known as the Carolingian Renaissance. Clear capital letters, spaces between words, question marks at the end of interrogative sentences—all of these patterns that are present in this very book were innovations introduced by Alcuin during the Carolingian Renaissance for the purpose of multiplying literacy.

Charlemagne was also intent upon bringing everyone into the Roman Church. When he conquered new territories, he forced all the residents to be baptized as Christians or else face death. Charlemagne standardized the liturgy of church worship and took it upon himself to appoint bishops. One historian has credited Charlemagne with making Europe "the new political order—nominally Christian, for better or for worse, for a thousand years" (Bruce L. Shelley). To be a "nominal Christian" means to be Christian in name only. In other words, even as someone claims the name of Jesus Christ, this person is not truly a follower of Jesus Christ—and so, ultimately, he or she is not actually a believer at all.

Using an encyclopedia or an Internet search, learn a little bit more about the Carolingian Renaissance. In the space below, list three specific aspects of the Carolingian Renaissance where you can see God's sovereign power at work in human history.

_____

_____

_____

_____

_____

_____

Now consider the "nominal Christianity" of the Middle Ages. How did a lack of training and discipleship affect the rise of nominal Christianity? How about a lack of literacy? How could Christian leaders in a largely illiterate culture have called people to authentic Christian commitment?

_____

_____

_____

_____

_____

Reforms from the Bishops of Rome

During the tenth century, the power of the popes increased—and so did corruption and scandal among popes, bishops, and priests! It wasn't until Pope Clement II in the eleventh century that the popes began to correct these abuses. Pope Clement II, as well as Pope Leo IX after him, tried to remove as much temptation as possible from the lives of popes, bishops, and priests.

One significant source of corruption was *simony*. Simony was the practice of purchasing positions of leadership in the church. The word "simony" comes from the name "Simon" in Acts 8. There, a man named Simon offered to pay Peter for the capacity to give people the Holy Spirit. Of course, no human being can give anyone a gift that comes only from God! When Peter placed his hands on Samaritans, Peter did not cause the Holy Spirit to dwell in them; Peter was simply recognizing publicly what God had already purposed to do. That's why, when Simon asked if he could purchase this power, Peter immediately rebuked him.

Pope Leo IX, also called "Bruno," recognized the deep problems and corruption caused by simony. At a gathering of bishops around Easter in the year 1049, Leo IX made it clear that any church leader who gained his role through simony was to be cut off from the church's communion.

In what ways may people today try to tie God's favor or God's gifts to money? Look up the article "Q & A: The Prosperity Gospel" at www.bpnews.net or "It Promises Far Too Little" at www.albertmohler.com. After reading one or both articles, read Acts 8:9–24. In what ways was Simon's view of God's gift similar to "prosperity gospel" thinking? In what ways was Simon's thinking different?

_____

_____

_____

_____

_____

At this same Easter gathering in 1049, Pope Leo IX revived an earlier tradition that had prohibited church leaders from marrying or engaging in sexual relations. As early as the fourth century, churches in some areas had required celibacy among church leaders. By the seventh century, churches in close fellowship with the Roman church typically prohibited married clergy; churches in the Eastern Empire frequently allowed married bishops and priests. In AD 692, a gathering of Eastern church leaders explicitly rejected the Roman pattern and allowed church leaders to be married: "We, preserving the ancient rule as well as the perfection and order of the apostles, affirm that lawful marriages of men in holy orders should be held steadfast from this time forward, by no means dissolving their union with their wives nor depriving them of mutual intercourse whenever it is convenient" (Quinisext Council). Leo IX, seeing that many bishops and priests were living in sexual sin, took the opposite approach; he required singleness and celibacy among Roman Catholic clergy.

Read 1 Timothy 3:1–7. In this passage, Paul provided God-inspired qualifications for bishops or overseers. Consider carefully the medieval prohibition that prevented marriage among priests, bishops, and popes of the Roman Catholic Church. Why did this prohibition seem like a good idea at the time? What may have been some positive benefits of unmarried church leaders? What potential problems might this prohibition have caused?

_____

_____

_____

_____

_____

_____

_____

Words from the Ones Who Were There

Alcuin of York

Alcuin of York, the Anglo-Saxon scholar appointed by Charlemagne to oversee a school in the city of Aix-la-Chapelle, once encouraged his students in their studies by exclaiming, "Ye lads whose age is fitted for reading, learn! The years go by like running water. Waste not the teachable days in idleness!"

What in your life would change this week if you truly took to heart the truth that "the years go by like running water"?

_____

_____

_____

_____

_____

Humbert of Rome

Humbert's letter, written in the name of the pope, excommunicated Eastern churches from fellowship with the Roman Catholic Church in the year 1054. In the letter, Humbert wrote, "Let them be *anathema maranatha* with ... all the heretics and with the devil himself and his angels, unless they should repent."

The Greek word *anathema* means "accursed" or "dedicated for destruction." *Maranatha* is an Aramaic term that means, "Master, come!" and referred to the future return of Jesus to earth. What Humbert declared was that, if Eastern churches did not repent and submit to the Roman church, they would be cursed when Jesus returned.

Study Galatians 1:6–9 and 1 Corinthians 16:22. At what point is it appropriate for a church leader to declare someone *"anathema maranatha"*?

_____

_____

_____

_____

_____

Pope Innocent III

"How, indeed, will the church of the Greeks ... return into ecclesiastical union and to a devotion for the apostolic seat?... Those who were supposed to be seeking the ends of Jesus Christ ... made their swords ... drip with Christian blood."

This was the response of Innocent III, bishop of Rome, when he heard about the Crusaders' tragic sack of Constantinople in 1204. He had called for the Fourth Crusade, as well as other Crusades intended to slaughter Muslims and heretics. What caused the bishop of Rome to think that the Crusades were actually "seeking the ends of Jesus Christ" in the first place? Why did he think that sacking Constantinople was inappropriate while sacking other cities would have supported "the ends of Jesus Christ"?

_____

_____

_____

_____

_____

What are the true "ends of Jesus Christ"? That is to say, what does Jesus truly desire as the goal for his people? Support your answer from Scripture.

_____

_____

_____

_____

Scriptural Responses to Conflicts in the Church and with the World

Possible Conflict Situation	Scriptural Response
I disagree with a brother or sister in Christ.	Eph. 4:1–16; Col. 3:12–17
A brother or sister in Christ is sinning.	Matt. 18:16–20; 1 Cor. 6:1–8; Gal. 6:1–5
I am speaking with someone who claims to be a Christian but who denies essential Christian beliefs.	Titus 3:1–11; 1 Peter 3:15–17
I am speaking with someone who isn't a Christian at all.	Matt. 28:16–20; 1 Peter 3:15–17

Family Time

Get Together: As a family, make a list of leaders. These can be political leaders, church leaders, past leaders, present leaders. In a fun way, perhaps by writing a rating between 1 and 10 on a paper and then holding up your ratings, give each leader a score. Discuss together how a truly great leader sees his or her role not as a lord, but as a servant first of God and then of people. Read Mark 10:45 and point to Jesus as the perfect leader.

Read Together: John 17:22–24

Learn Together: On the night before Jesus was crucified, he talked to God the Father about all the people who would trust in him (John 17). And what did he pray for us? He prayed that his people would work together in oneness so that the watching world would trust in Jesus.

Many times throughout the history of Christianity, church leaders weren't servant leaders. They looked for ways to strengthen their own churches or their own positions. One result of this pattern was division between the churches in the Eastern Empire and the churches closer to the city of Rome. At one point, a crusader army from the western, Roman side destroyed the beautiful city of Constantinople and murdered thousands of Eastern citizens.

Christians today may not send crusader armies against other churches. But sometimes we use words and actions to tear down other people and other churches. How can we speak the undiluted truth about God and the gospel while seeking the oneness that Jesus prayed for?

Pray Together: "God our Father, help us to respond more completely to what you have already accomplished for us through Jesus Christ, the ultimate example of powerful meekness and righteous love. Grant us compassion toward others. Work in us, through your Spirit, the longing to rest in your righteousness even in times of conflict. In the name of Jesus Christ our Lord, Amen."

SESSION 6
God's Work Goes On
AD *500–1300*

The church in the Middle Ages was mired in corruption and controversy. Looking back, it can sometimes seem like proclamation of the gospel was completely lost. Yet was it? During this era, missionaries like Cyril and Methodius spread the message of Jesus to unreached lands. Scholars like Thomas Aquinas changed the way people looked at God's creation. Monks like Bernard of Clairvaux called people to a radical love for God, and Peter Waldo laid the foundations for future reforms. Despite the failures of his people, God's work rolled on.

Session 6 Outline

1. Missionaries

    a. Boniface and Lioba became missionaries to the Germans (716)

    b. Brothers Cyril and Methodius became missionaries to Slavic peoples (862).

2. Reformers

    a. Berno established a monastery at Cluny that sparked a revival (910).

    b. Bernard of Clairvaux called people to a deeper love of God (1115).

3. Mendicants

    a. Peter Waldo and the "poor folk" challenged church authority (1179).

    b. Francis of Assisi took a vow of poverty (1205).

4. Dominicans

    a. Thomas Aquinas brought together Aristotle's philosophy and Catholic theology in his *Summa Theologica* (1266).

Key Terms

Abbot – (from *abba*, "father") Leader in a monastic community, particularly a community that follows the Rule of Benedict.

Dominican Order – Order of Friars Preachers, founded by Dominic in the thirteenth century. Dominicans have a strong intellectual history and include notable figures such as Thomas Aquinas and Bartolome de las Casas.

Franciscans – Order of Friars Minor, founded by Francis of Assisi in the early thirteenth century. Many Franciscans have been traveling monks who model the life of Francis, including wearing plain brown robes and ropes around their waists like Francis did.

Francis of Assisi (1182–1226)

Friar – (From French, *frère*, "brother") Member of a Roman Catholic mendicant order.

Mendicants – (Latin, "beggar") Order of monks who preach, own no property, and serve the poor.

Monastery – Also known as an Abbey, the place of residence for communities of nuns or monks.

Pontiff or pontifex – (from Latin, "high priest") Beginning in the Middle Ages, a title for the bishop of Rome.

Monastery in Cluny, France

Purgatory – Roman Catholic teaching about an intermediate state of being where souls of the dead can be purged of sins and thereby become ready to enter heaven.

Scholasticism – Method for reasoning that arose in Middle Ages and tried to bring together Christian theology and Greek philosophy.

Waldensians – Also known as the Poor Folk of Lyons, they were followers of Peter Waldo in France in the twelfth century. They were persecuted for preaching without the authorization of the Roman Catholic Church.

Know More About...

God's Work in the Middle Ages

So many ungodly circumstances marked the churches in the Middle Ages. That's one of the reasons why it's easy to forget that God really was at work in this era.

Jesus saw clearly that his Father never stopped working, even when his own people were rejecting him (John 5:17). If God the Father was at work even when God the Son was being rejected and crucified, there is no time or place so dark that God isn't working for his own glory and for the good of his people.

In the Middle Ages, God was clearly at work in monastic missions, the renewal of monastic orders, the proliferation of preaching among mendicants, and the faithfulness of Scholastic scholars.

This doesn't mean, of course, that everyone involved these movements was always obedient to God's Word. Truth be told, it's quite probable that many monks, mendicants, and Scholastics were not authentic followers of Jesus or that their thinking about God was confused. Yet God worked through each of these movements to preserve and to spread his Word.

Renewals in Orders of Monks and Nuns

Monasteries and convents began as communities for men and women who longed to leave the world's temptations and to devote themselves to study and service. In time, well-positioned families came to see donations to monasteries as a pathway to positioning their souls in God's good favor. As a result, monasteries became not only centers for divine study but also repositories for the world's wealth.

In the closing years of the eleventh century, a band of Benedictine monks abandoned their jewel-adorned monastery to seek a simpler monastic life in the French valley of Cistertium, also known as Citeaux. Because of their roots in the region of Cistertium, they became known as Cistercian monks. So strict was the Cistercian rule that, to avoid any appearance of wealth, the monks even refused to dye their robes. Still today, Cistercians wear white robes.

By 1112, there was a problem among the Cistercian monks, though: No one was joining their community. The lifestyle was simply too strict. The dispirited leader of the community was preparing to quit when someone called out from the gate. When he arrived at the gate, he was awestruck. Not one, not five, not ten, but thirty-one men stood at the gate! All of them wanted to become monks.

When it comes to dealing with money and other assets that the world sees as valuable, what could your church learn from the experiences of medieval monks and nuns?

_____

_____

_____

_____

_____

Preaching among the Mendicants

Especially in the early Middle Ages, preaching was typically a task reserved for bishops. Laypeople had little access to the Bible. People seeking an encounter with God through Scripture could do so only through Bible readings at church—and then only if they understood Latin!

With the rise of the mendicants, preaching shifted from the pulpits to the streets. Mendicants were traveling preachers who taught the Scriptures and served the poor. Some mendicants were church-authorized monks while others were God-called laypeople.

One man who gave up his profession as a merchant to become a mendicant preacher was Peter Waldo (sometimes spelled "Valdes"). Waldo never became a bishop, a monk, or even a priest. Yet, in the 1170s, he sold his personal possessions and committed himself to a life of giving to others and explaining the Scriptures to anyone who would listen. Waldo's followers became known as "the Poor Folk of Lyons" in his lifetime and as "Waldensians" in later years.

In 1179, the pope declared that no one could publicly interpret Scripture without the permission of their local bishop. But Waldo and his followers kept preaching the biblical text in the language of the common people whenever and wherever people would listen. Threatened with excommunication, Peter Waldo simply replied, "We must obey God rather than men" (Acts 5:29). The pope identified the Waldensians as dangerous heretics, and at least eighty Waldensians were burned for their beliefs. This martyrdom marked the beginning of several centuries of persecution that nearly destroyed the Waldensian movement.

Study Paul's words to Timothy in 2 Timothy 3:16–4:2. Notice how Paul moved directly from an affirmation of the inspiration of Scripture to clear instructions about preaching Scripture faithfully.

In many regions in the Middle Ages, the inspiration of Scripture was accepted but Scripture was not proclaimed, and, as a result, the message of the Scriptures remained unknown. Read Romans 10:14–17.

In the space below, answer these questions: What happens when understandable preaching ceases to be a central part of a church's worship? What should be central purpose of a sermon? What should provide the primary content of a sermon?

_____

_____

_____

_____

_____

The Scholastics

The method of learning known as Scholasticism arose as Christian scholars worked to resolve contradictions between the divine Scriptures, the church's theology, and pagan philosophy.

Alcuin of York and Anselm of Canterbury laid many of the foundations for Scholasticism, but they weren't really full-fledged Scholastics. The founders of Scholasticism were scholars like Peter Abelard. Abelard developed his summaries of Christian theology from a foundation of human reason. Abelard's reliance on human reason more than divine revelation led to several clashes between him and Bernard of Clairvaux. Scholastics after Abelard not only rooted their theology in reason, but also looked for points of contact between Muslim philosophy and Christian theology.

In the thirteenth century, Thomas Aquinas emerged as the greatest of the Scholastics. Earlier Scholastics had focused on the writings of Augustine and on modifications of the Greek philosopher Plato. Thomas interacted with these sources but he leaned far more heavily on the philosophy of Aristotle. At the same time, he, unlike many other Scholastics, kept his philosophy tightly tethered to the traditions of the church and to God's revelation of himself in Scripture.

Scholasticism looked for points of contact between pagan philosophy and God's revelation of himself through Scripture, church tradition, and creation. God's creation includes orderliness that even non-believers can recognize and categorize into philosophical systems. What can Christians learn from these non-Christian philosophies? What are the dangers of drawing wisdom from non-Christian worldviews?

_____

_____

_____

_____

_____

Words from the Ones Who Were There

Boniface

The missionary monk Boniface, when he and his fellow monks were faced with death, told them, "Sons, cease fighting. Lay down your arms, for we are told in Scripture not to render evil for good but to overcome evil by good. The hour to which we have long looked forward is near and the day of our release is at hand. Take comfort in the Lord and endure with gladness the suffering he has mercifully ordained. Put your faith in him and he will grant deliverance to your souls."

Study Matthew 5:38–48. Locate and read the article "Jim Elliot: No Fool" on www.christianity.com. More than 1,000 years separate the death of Boniface and his companions from the death of Jim Elliot and his fellow missionaries. Yet both stories are strikingly similar: for the sake of the gospel, missionaries chose to obey Jesus by embracing death instead of injuring their attackers. These missionaries' calling to proclaim the gospel was more important to them than their own lives.

How can you rest so fully in the sufficiency of Jesus that you are willing to let go of your life and dreams for the sake of the gospel?

_____

_____

_____

_____

_____

Family Time

Get Together: Talk with your family members about several subjects that they are studying or have studied in school. Ask about their hardest subjects and easiest subjects, most fun subjects and least enjoyable subjects. As you discuss each subject, consider how this subject points to the orderliness with which God created the world in the beginning.

Read Together: Colossians 1:15–17

Learn Together: Because God created an orderly world, even people who are not Christians can recognize God's orderliness in subjects like science and medicine and philosophy. In these subjects and in many others, non-Christians may reject the real source of the orderliness that they see, but they are still able to make sense of these subjects because of the orderliness with which God created the world. According to the apostle Paul, the orderliness of the world only comes together and makes sense because of Jesus. The world ultimately makes sense only when we see Jesus as the one who holds it all together.

Scholastic thinkers like Thomas Aquinas recognized that non-Christian philosophers could provide some wisdom. Yet Thomas also recognized that the dim light of pagan philosophy was never enough to lead people to know God in his fullness. On December 6, 1273, Thomas attended an observance of the Lord's Supper. No one knows exactly what happened during that worship service, but Thomas seems to have experienced God in a way that not even he could put into words. After he left the chapel, he said, "All that I have written seems to me nothing but straw, compared to what I have seen and what has been revealed to me."

Pray Together: "Heavenly Father, thank you for preserving your light in the world, even in the darkest of times. Your promises are everlasting. Every question we have will someday find its answer in you. Help us to always seek you first, in every situation, so that, through our questions, you may strengthen our faith. Amen."

SESSION 7
Everything Falls Apart
AD *1300–1500*

Enormous tragedies in the fourteenth and fifteenth centuries challenged people's trust in God. Three popes at once vied for the papacy, the Hundred Years' War and the Black Death took millions of lives across Europe, and Muslim Turks conquered what was left of the Eastern Empire. But in the midst of this, God raised up fresh voices, like John Wycliffe in England and Jan Hus in Bohemia, to turn people's minds to the Scriptures and the beauty of the gospel. A renaissance in learning was sparked by classical manuscripts and Gutenberg's printing press. Seeds of reform had been planted and were about to take root among God's people.

Session 7 Outline

1. Popes away from Rome

    a. Pope Boniface VIII issued the "Unam Sanctum" (1302).

    b. Popes resided near French border for 72 years (1305–1377).

2. The Hundred Years' War (1337–1453)

3. The Plague (Black Death) (mid-1300s)

4. Corruption and Division

    a. Catherine of Siena convinced the pope to return to Rome (1377).

    b. Two popes elected: One in Rome and a French pope in Avignon (1378).

    c. Council of Pisa resulted in three popes (1409).

5. Renewal of Gospel Proclamation

    a. John Wycliffe translated the Bible into English (1382).

    b. Jan Hus in Bohemia challenged the Roman Catholic Church's authority.

    c. Council of Constance executed Hus, burned Wycliffe's bones, and established one pope (1414–1418).

6. Renewal in Classical Learning

    a. Ottoman Turks conquered Constantinople (1453); Classical texts from Constantinople taken to the West.

    b. Renaissance humanism

    c. Gutenberg's printing press (1440)

    d. Erasmus' Greek New Testament (1516)

Key Terms

Babylonian Captivity of the Church – Also called "Babylonian Captivity of the Papacy," refers to the 72 years in the fourteenth century in which the popes resided not in Rome, but in France. It began in 1305 when Clement V was elected pope but refused to move to Rome and instead stayed in Avignon, France. It ended in 1377 when Pope Gregory XI returned to Rome at the urging of Catherine of Siena.

Council of Constance (1414-1418) – Deposed the three popes who claimed the title and elected a new pope, ending the papal schism; declared Jan Hus a heretic and burned him at the stake; declared the late John Wycliffe a heretic and burned his remains.

Council of Pisa (1409) – Deposed the two popes that claimed the title and elected a third pope. However the legitimacy of this council was disputed and the popes refused to give up their title, thus resulting in three popes. This paved the way for the Council of Constance a few years later.

Humanists – Instead of emphasizing theoretical knowledge, humanists during the Renaissance emphasized practical engagement in the civic life of their communities. They valued the study of grammar, public speaking, history, poetry, and philosophy. Notable humanists included Francesco Petrarch, Leonardo da Vinci, and Desiderius Erasmus.

Erasmus of Rotterdam (1466–1536)

Hundred Years' War (1337-1453) – War between England and France in which the French eventually succeeded in expelling the English from France, but only after more than 100 years of bloody battles. The French peasant girl Joan of Arc lead several successful battles for France in this war.

Renaissance – Revival of ancient classical learning and art, beginning in the fourteenth and fifteenth centuries. Renaissance humanism emphasized practical learning and challenged the Scholasticism of the Middle Ages which focused on theoretical knowledge.

Scholasticism – Method for reasoning that arose in Middle Ages and tried to bring together Christian theology and Greek philosophy, particularly the philosophy of Aristotle. Some of the primary Scholastic thinkers were Anselm of Canterbury, Peter Abelard, and Thomas Aquinas.

Unam Sanctum (1302) – (Latin, "the one holy") A papal bull issued by Pope Boniface VIII which lays out the position of the pope as the supreme head of the church and the necessity of belonging to the church in order to have eternal salvation.

Know More About...

When faced with a valley of dry bones, Ezekiel was instructed to speak the words of God to the bones. When he did, the bones came to life! (Ezek. 37)

Perhaps more than any other time in human history, the later Middle Ages and early Renaissance eras represent a time that seemed spiritually dry. I am reminded of the repeated phrase in the book of Judges: "In those days there was no king in Israel; every man did what was right in his own eyes" (17:6; 21:25). The Israelites failed to recognize God as their ultimate King and as the only One who could provide them with the right kind of human kings.

Something similar happened in this era of church history: Many people failed to recognize Jesus as the true and only rightful ruler of his church (Eph. 5:23). And what was the result? Three popes at the same time! One of the biggest church splits in history! Decreasing confidence in the church among the people! Those were the events that characterized the fourteenth through the early sixteenth centuries.

The Plague

History demonstrates that little things in life can make a huge difference! Although it's hard to believe that a disease carried by a flea could bring about the death of nearly one-third of an entire population, that is exactly what happened in Europe in the mid-1300s. This disease, called the Bubonic Plague or Black Death, was transmitted by fleas on disease-infested rats carried on cargo ships.

Not only did this terrible plague kill nearly 24 million people, it also helped to trigger fear and skepticism among the people of Europe, which had an impact on the next two centuries of Christian history. Because the plague overtook even those who appeared to be healthy, fear was everywhere. People lived in fear of the plague, fear of hell, and fear of a God who would judge them all. It caused people to question God's goodness and to wonder whether the established church was telling them the truth about God. Unfortunately, instead of proclaiming the gospel, many church leaders were merely calling people to follow the church's teachings and to be good. As a result, there was little hope of comfort for most people.

When faced with fearful circumstance, how do you respond? How can you develop a habit of trusting more completely in the goodness of God no matter what the circumstance?

_____

_____

_____

_____

The Power of the Press

Johannes Gutenberg's refinement of the printing press in 1440 provided an avenue for the resurgence of the biblical literacy—and the world has never been the same. Most of you reading these words own several printed Bibles—not to mention the fact that you may have Bibles on your smartphone or ebook reader as well!

One of the key results of Gutenberg's movable metal-type printing press was that the average person became less dependent on the established church for information. More and more people were able to read the Scriptures for themselves.

Replica of Gutenberg's Printing Press

What would be different in your life today if you did not have access to the Bible?

_____

_____

_____

_____

_____

With Bibles so abundant nowadays, it's all too easy for us to take the Bible for granted. What are some specific ways that you may have taken the availability of the Bible for granted?

_____

_____

_____

_____

The Great Papal Schism

In the late fourteenth century, one of the biggest church divisions in history took place. It was during this time that two different popes were claiming to be the rightful successor of the apostle Peter. The issue resulted in each pope (Urban VI in Rome and Clement VII in Avignon) refusing to abdicate his position. To further complicate the power struggle, Pope Alexander V was elected as bishop of Rome in 1409, resulting in three different popes claiming to be the successor of the apostle Peter! It was not until the Council of Constance in 1415 that this controversy ended. These events contributed to concerns among the laypeople of Europe about the nature of the church. This time period caused many to wonder if what they were being taught was the correct view of the church.

In your own words, explain what "the church" is according to the New Testament.

_____

_____

_____

_____

If you were asked to describe your local church, what words would you use?

_____

_____

_____

_____

Words from the Ones Who Were There

William Langland

William Langland, a fourteenth-century poet, described the era in which he lived like this: "So Nature killed many through corruptions,/Death came driving after her and dashed all to dust,/Kings and knights, emperors and popes./... For God is deaf nowadays and will not hear us,/And for our guilt he grinds good men to dust."

Take a minute to think back through the events in the fourteenth century. If you had a two-minute ride on an elevator with William Langland, what would you ask him?

_____

_____

_____

_____

_____

_____

_____

_____

John Wycliffe

John Wycliffe, who translated the Bible into common English, said, "Englishmen learn Christ's law best in English. Moses heard God's law in his own tongue; so did Christ's apostles."

This same mindset has been carried forward by thousands of missionaries who desire to translate the Bible into people groups' native tongue. One of these groups, called Wycliffe Bible Translators, has translated the Bible into over 700 languages, but much work is yet to be done.

John Wycliffe (1328–1384)

List three specific ways that you might support the work of Bible translation throughout the world:

1. _____

_____

_____

2. _____

_____

_____

3. _____

_____

_____

Pope Boniface VIII

In 1302 in the papal bull *Unam Sanctum*, Pope Boniface VIII issued this statement: "The gospel teaches us that ... the Church has in her power, two swords, the spiritual and the temporal; both are in the power of the Church; but the first must be drawn by the Church, and by the arm of the sovereign pontiff; the second, for the Church, by the arm of the kings and soldiers at the pontiff's request. The temporal sword ought to be subject to the spiritual."

Read Ephesians 4:7–16 and Acts 2:40–47. How do the words of Pope Boniface VIII compare with your understanding of the teachings of Scripture about the church?

_____

_____

_____

_____

_____

_____

_____

_____

Family Time

Get Together: At one of the darkest times in human history the light of God's Word provided guidance and truth. David sang, "Your word is a lamp to my feet and a light to my path" (Ps. 119:105). In this session we can see how God preserves his people even through death, church divisions, and corrupt leadership. Amidst all of darkness and devastation, God's Word stands as not only as a symbol of hope but also as God's chosen instrument to convey his truth to the world. This truth was so important to Jan Hus that he refused to compromise his proclamation, even in the face of death.

Talk about the following question: Have you ever been treated unfairly because of your faith in Jesus Christ?

Read Together: Read 2 Corinthians 4:7–11.

Learn Together: It was Jan Hus who said, "The pope is not the head, nor are the cardinals the whole body of the holy. Only Christ is the head of the church, his predestined ones are the body, and each one of them is a member of that body." It was because of this and similar statements that on July 6, 1415, Jan Hus was burned alive.

His death did not mark the end of his teachings. Hus's followers continued to carry on his message of calling people back to a biblical view of the church. Years later, the written words of Jan Hus inspired Martin Luther to proclaim the gospel anew.

Discuss together what beliefs or ideals for which you would be willing to sacrifice everything.

Pray Together: "Heavenly Father, thank you for your Word, and its power to change my life, and the life of my family. Today I renew my commitment to be faithful to you in the little things of life. Today I renew my commitment to you and your Word. Today I renew my commitment to allowing you to define and lead your church. In Jesus' name, I ask these things. Amen."

SESSION 8
The Reformation
AD *1500–1600*

So many influences came together in the sixteenth century to bring about gospel renewal in Europe. Wycliffe and Hus had packed a powder keg. Erasmus had woven a fuse. On October 31, 1517, a hotheaded monk named Martin Luther lit the fuse and rocked the world.

Soon after, other reformers, like John Calvin and William Tyndale, in defiance of church and state authorities didn't let up in their mission to spread the Word of God to peasant and noble alike. Meanwhile, a radical group known as the Anabaptists arose and began to press the limits even further.

Session 8 Outline

1. How reformation began with the righteousness of God.

    a. Martin Luther:

        i.   Became a monk and sought righteousness (Ps. 31:1; Rom. 1:17).

        ii. Posted 95 Theses to protest the sale of indulgences (October 31, 1517).

        iii. Defended his writings at the Diet of Worms (1521).

    b. John Calvin wrote *Institutes of the Christian Religion* in Geneva, Switzerland.

    c. Ulrich Zwingli challenged church practices in Zurich, Switzerland.

2. How reformation turned radical.

    a. Anabaptist Felix Manz became the first Protestant martyred by other Protestants (1527).

    b. Menno Simons led a group of Anabaptists who later became known as Mennonites.

3. How reformation reached England.

    a. William Tyndale translated the New Testament into common English (1525).

4. How reformation looked in the Roman Catholic Church.

    a. Colloquy of Regensburg failed to unify Catholics and Protestants (1541).

    b. Ignatius Loyola founded the Society of Jesus (Jesuit Order).

    c. Council of Trent (1545–1563):

        i.   Denied justification by faith alone.

        ii. Affirmed that the elements of the Lord's Supper become the body and blood of Jesus Christ.

        iii. Proclaimed that the Bible is to be interpreted according to and with church tradition.

Key Terms

Anabaptists – (from Greek, "again-baptizer") They taught—contrary to infant baptism—that only believers should be baptized ("believers' baptism") and that the state should not enforce religious beliefs. Mennonites, Quakers, and the Amish have their roots in the Anabaptist movement.

Colloquy of Regensburg (1541) – Conference held in Regensburg, Germany to bring Protestants and Catholics together. But after weeks of theological debate, the conference ended in a stalemate.

Council of Trent (1545-1563) – After the failed attempt at unity in the Colloquy of Regensburg, the Catholic Church at the Council of Trent formally rejected Protestant teachings.

Indulgences – In Roman Catholic theology, it's a release from the temporal (earthly) penalties that a person must endure to demonstrate repentance from his or her sins.

Ignatius Loyola (1491–1556)

Jesuit Order – Religious order founded by Ignatius of Loyola in the sixteenth century. Today, Jesuits are one of the largest religious orders of the Catholic Church. They are known for their missionary work, social justice, and colleges and universities.

Lutherans – Protestant denomination emerging from the work of Martin Luther in the sixteenth century. Lutherans today number more than 60 million worldwide.

Mennonites – Anabaptist group founded by Menno Simons in the sixteenth century. Today, Mennonites are the largest of the Anabaptist groups. They are sometimes known as "peace churches" because of their emphasis on non-violence and pacifism.

Menno Simons (1496–1561)

Protestants – Groups during the Reformation that rejected the supreme authority of the pope later became known as Protestants. Today, Protestants include denominations such as Lutherans, Presbyterians, Anglicans, and many others.

Purgatory – Roman Catholic teaching about an intermediate state of death where souls can be purged of sins and thereby become ready to enter heaven.

Solas – (from Latin, "alone") Five statements that summarize the Reformation understanding of salvation: *sola fide* (salvation is through faith alone), *sola gratia* (salvation is by God's grace alone), *sola Scriptura* (written witness to God's way of salvation is Scripture alone), *solus Christus* (salvation is in Christ alone), *soli Deo gloria* (salvation is for God's glory alone).

Transubstantiation – In Roman Catholic teaching, transubstantiation is a way of explaining how Christ is truly present in the bread and wine of the Lord's Supper. The substance of the elements—which is invisible—becomes the blood and body of Jesus, while the visible things of the elements—such as shape, taste, color, texture—remain unchanged.

Know More About...

"But when the fullness of the time came, God sent forth His Son" (Gal. 4:4). Jesus came to earth on God's timetable and in God's way! The many events that came together in the sixteenth century demonstrate the goodness of God's sovereign timing.

The Importance of Theology

The word theology means "ideas or thoughts" (-logy) "about God" (theo-). The Reformation was a deeply theological movement. It began with Martin Luther's Ninety-Five Theses, which were topics for theological debate. It continued with a theological textbook, John Calvin's Institutes of the Christian Religion. Along the way, the Reformation was fueled by theological debates that not only scholars but also lay-people heard. In fact, if only a few scholars in universities had embraced the Reformation message, the Reformation would likely have had no lasting effect! The success of the Reformation required not only scholars but also thousands of people from a variety of backgrounds to dig into Scripture, learn more, and teach theology to others.

List three reasons why the study of theology is important for every Christian:

1. _____

_____

_____

2. _____

_____

_____

3. _____

_____

_____

The English Bible

Standing on the shoulders of those who had gone before him, William Tyndale took the work of John Wycliffe and Desiderius Erasmus a step further with his desire to put the Bible into the hands of ordinary people. It was Tyndale who told a priest, "If God spares my life, I will cause the plowboy to know more about Scripture than you do!" Tyndale's work laid the foundation for the King James Version, which was first published in 1611.

In the book of Acts, Christians in Berea were commended for receiving "the word with great eagerness, examining the Scriptures daily to see whether these things [the teachings of Paul] were so" (Acts 17:11). How can Christians today recognize the leadership of their church leaders while pursuing their God-given responsibility to search the Scriptures for themselves?

_____

_____

_____

_____

_____

_____

How to Change the World

The following lines may be as old as the twelfth century AD:

> "When I was a young man, I wanted to change the world.
> I found it was difficult to change the world, so I tried to change my nation.
> When I found I couldn't change the nation, I began to focus on my town.
> I couldn't change the town and as an older man, I tried to change my family.
> Now, as an old man, I realize the only thing I can change is myself, and suddenly I realize that if long ago I had changed myself, I could have made an impact on my family.
> My family and I could have made an impact on our town.
> Their impact could have changed the nation and I could indeed have changed the world."

—Author Unknown

Transformation of entire societies can begin with transformation in one person's heart. Consider Martin Luther's recognition that he could be made right with God only by grace through faith in Jesus! Or what about William Tyndale's declaration that he would make sure that the plowboy could someday read the Bible in ordinary English? In each case, personal transformation affected an entire society.

How is God calling you to respond to his work of transformation in your heart right now?

_____

_____

_____

_____

_____

_____

_____

What if the power of gospel of Jesus transformed your city or your neighborhood? How would your community look different?

_____

_____

_____

_____

_____

_____

Words from the Ones Who Were There

Martin Luther

Speaking against the abuse of the indulgence system Martin Luther said, "They preach only human doctrines who say that as soon as the money clinks into the money chest, the soul [leaps] out of purgatory.... It is certain that when money clinks in the money chest, greed and avarice can be increased; but when the church intercedes, the result is in the hands of God alone" (Luther's Ninety-five Theses).

Martin Luther (1483–1546)

Have you ever been placed in a situation like Luther where you knew you had to stand for the truth of Scripture, even if you might face backlash? Describe the situation and your response below:

_____

_____

_____

_____

_____

_____

_____

John Calvin

John Calvin warned fellow Christians, "Beware lest our words and thoughts go beyond what the Word of God tells us.... We must leave to God his own knowledge ... and understand him as he makes himself known to us, without attempting to discover anything about his nature apart from his Word."

How do people today sometimes try to discover the nature of God "apart from his Word"? What is the danger in this?

_____

_____

_____

_____

_____

_____

_____

John Calvin (1509–1564)

Family Time

Get Together: The sixteenth century was marked by three principles that revealed a deep divide between the Reformers and the leaders of the Roman Catholic Church: (1) justification by faith, (2) supremacy of Scripture, and (3) priesthood of all believers.

These important differences had an impact on Christian worship and practices. One particular area that was affected was the issue of baptism. There were also disagreements among Protestants about who should be baptized and when.

Talk as a family about your experiences of baptism. Were you baptized as an infant or as a believer? What is your church's understanding of right timing and practice for baptism?

Read Together: Matthew 28:19, Acts 8:36, and Acts 16:32–33.

Learn Together: Martin Luther, John Calvin, and Ulrich Zwingli practiced infant baptism. Certain followers of Zwingli, however, disagreed. Convinced that the Bible taught that only believers should be baptized, the followers of Zwingli baptized themselves, earning the name "again-baptizers," or "Anabaptists."

Discuss these different perspectives on baptism with your children. Help them to understand the practices in your church. Help them also to see that faithful Christians disagree about the timing and the mode of baptism.

Pray Together: Some scholars believe that 2 Timothy 2:11–13 was an ancient hymn that Christians sang when new converts were baptized. Share this prayer based on these scripture verses: "God our Father, through baptism, we declare that we have died with your Son and that, because he has put to death the power of our sinful natures, we will live forever with him. Work in us by your Spirit so that we will endure to the end and will never deny the work of your Son. Help us to rest in the truth that, even when our faith fails, you are faithful still. In the name of Jesus Christ our Lord, Amen."

SESSION 9

Post-Reformation Growing Pains

*AD **1600–1700***

The seventeenth century was an era in flux. The church had fractured into a myriad of Protestant groups across Europe. The new congregations struggled over theological issues like predestination, infant baptism, and the relationship between church and state. Puritans wanted to purify the Church of England, while Separatists left and started their own congregations.

Though discovery of the Americas opened up possibilities to spread the gospel, the New World quickly became marred by the exploitation of natives and the importation of African slaves. Courageous believers like Bartolome de las Casas and William Wilberforce would spend their lives fighting this terrible injustice.

Session 9 Outline

1. Clashes between Protestants and Catholics

    a. Defenestration of Prague (1618)

    b. Thirty Years' War (1618–1648)

2. Clashes among Protestants

    a. Jacob Arminius disputed Calvinism's view of predestination.

    b. Synod of Dort sided with Calvinism (1618).

3. Conflicts in England

    a. Puritans tried to purify the Church of England by presenting the Millenary Petition to King James I (1603).

    b. King James Bible was published (1611).

c. Westminster Assembly was called to restructure the Church of England (1643–1649).

d. Oliver Cromwell allowed different Christian groups to worship freely.

e. Separatists wanted to separate from the Church of England.

　　i. John Smyth led the first English Baptists.

　　ii. John Bunyan wrote *The Pilgrim's Progress* (1678).

4. Clashes in the New World

a. Bartolome de las Casas campaigned against the encomienda system (1545).

b. Pedro Claver, "always a slave of the Africans" (1622).

c. William Wilberforce worked to abolish the British slave trade.

Key Terms

Arminianism – (named for Jacob Arminius) Belief that God gives every human being the gift (known as "prevenient grace") of being able to decide on their own whether to trust Jesus when they hear the gospel. God foresaw which individuals would choose to trust Jesus, and God planned in eternity past to save and to regenerate those individuals in response to their choice to trust Jesus.

Baptists – Christians who accept baptism of believers only and who view each local congregation of believers as autonomous. John Smyth (1570–1612) is often considered the first English Baptist.

Calvinism – (named for John Calvin; also called Reformed theology) Belief that, because human beings are dead in their sins, no one will choose to trust Jesus for salvation unless they are first regenerated ("born again") by God's Spirit. God planned in eternity past ("predestined") to regenerate particular individuals. When those who are predestined are born anew and hear the gospel, they respond to God's work in their lives by trusting Jesus for salvation.

Defenestration of Prague (1618) – An assembly of Protestants in Prague concluded that Roman Catholic leaders were guilty of closing Protestant churches in Bohemia. At the assembly, the Protestants threw the Catholic envoys out the window. Although the Catholic envoys survived the fall, this incident was one of several events that triggered the Thirty Years' War between Catholics and Protestants.

Encomienda System – The exploitation of natives on plantations in the Americas, particularly by the Spanish settlers.

Hampton Court Conference (1604) – Meeting between King James I of England and the Puritans in response to the Millenary Petition. Puritan concerns about English Bible translations discussed at this conference led to King James I calling for a new translation of the Bible; this translation later became known as the King James Version.

King James Bible (1611) – Also called the Authorized Version, King James I of England initiated this translation in 1604 after the Hampton Court Conference. The translation was completed in 1611 and became the standard Bible used in the Church of England.

Millenary Petition (1603) – Letter signed by 1,000 Puritan leaders given to King James I of England requesting, among other items: (1) simpler Sunday worship services in the Book of Common Prayer, (2) pastors that were "able and sufficient" preachers, (3) bishops to be no longer provided with multiple residences, and (4) church discipline administered according to New Testament.

Puritans – Protestants in sixteenth- and seventeenth-century England who wanted to purify the Church of England by reviving New Testament patterns of worship. Some Puritans from England sailed to America and settled the Massachusetts Bay Colony around the year 1630.

Separatists – Protestants in sixteenth- and seventeenth-century England who separated from the Church of England and formed independent congregations. One group of Separatists, originally from England, sailed to America and founded Plymouth Colony in Massachusetts in 1620.

Synod of Dort (1618) – Assembly of the Reformed Church in Dort, Netherlands that addressed the issue of Arminianism. The assembly rejected Arminianism and produced the Canons of Dort outlining Reformed (Calvinist) beliefs.

Thirty Years' War (1618–1648) – A conflict primarily between Protestant nations and Roman Catholic nations, beginning with the Defenestration of Prague and ending with the Peace of Westphalia.

Westminster Assembly (1643–1649) – Gathering of church leaders in England to reorganize the Church of England. The assembly produced the Westminster Confession of Faith in 1646.

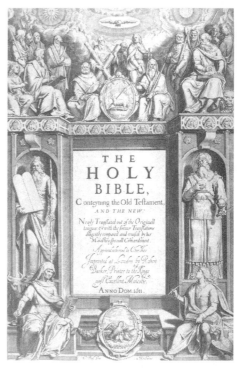

Title Page of the 1611 King James Bible

Arminianism and Calvinism

Issue	Arminianism (The Remonstrance)	Calvinism, Reformed Theology (The Canons of Dort)
Predestination John 6:44; 15:16; Rom. 9:10–16	**Conditional predestination.** God observed from eternity past who would believe, then God predestined people according to this foresight. *"God, by an eternal, unchangeable purpose in Jesus Christ ... before the foundation of the world, ... determined ... to save ... those who ... shall believe on this his Son Jesus, and shall persevere." (Arminian Remonstrance, Article I)*	**Unconditional predestination.** God predestined people to be saved not because he foresaw any good choices in them but simply because of his grace. *"Before the foundation of the world, by sheer grace, ... God chose in Christ to salvation a definite number of particular people. ... This election took place, not on the basis of foreseen faith ... but rather for the purpose of faith." (Canons of Dort, I)*
Atonement Job 42:1-2; John 10:14–15, 28; 1 John 2:2	**Indefinite atonement.** Jesus obtained redemption for every human being, but these people can refuse to believe and, whenever someone does refuse, God's work of redemption is thwarted in that person's life. *"Jesus Christ ...died for all men and for every man, so that he has obtained for them all ... redemption, and the forgiveness of sins; yet that no one actually enjoys this forgiveness of sins, except the believer." (Article II)*	**Definite atonement.** Though the atoning sacrifice of Jesus was sufficient to redeem the whole world, this death purchased the salvation only of those whom God in his grace chose before time. *"This death of God's Son is ... more than sufficient to atone for the sins of the whole world. ... It was God's will that Christ through the blood of the cross ... should effectively redeem from every people, tribe, nation, and language all those and only those who were chosen from eternity to salvation and given to him by the Father." (Canons, II)*
Human Nature Ps. 14:2–3; 53:2–3; Rom. 3:10–12; Eph. 2:1–3	**Defective human nature.** Although people will not do anything good in their own power, enough grace remains in every human to choose faith in Jesus. *"Man ... of and by himself can neither think, will, nor do anything that is truly good; ... it is needful that he be born again of God in Christ, through his Holy Spirit." (Article III)*	**Radically corrupted human nature.** Humanity's fallenness is so great that no one naturally desires to submit to God or to trust in Jesus. *"All people are conceived in sin and are born children of wrath, ... neither willing nor able to return to God." (Canons, III/IV)*

Issue	Arminianism	Calvinism
Grace John 6:37, 44; Eph. 2:4–6	**Resistible grace.** When God's Spirit works in a sinner to bring about the new birth, the sinner can reject God's attempts to bring new life. *"As respects the mode of the operation of this grace, it is not irresistible, inasmuch as it is written concerning many that they have resisted the Holy Ghost." (Article IV)*	**Effective grace.** Though people do resist the Holy Spirit up to the time when God brings about new life in them, God transforms the person at the time of the new birth (or regeneration) so that he or she desires to trust Jesus and actually does believe. *"Regeneration ... is an entirely supernatural work. ... All those in whose hearts God works in this marvelous way are certainly, unfailingly, and effectively reborn and do actually believe." (Canons, III/IV)*
Perseverance John 10:27–28; Rom. 8:29–39	**Perseverance dependent on the believer's will and work.** Scripture does not clearly state whether a Christian can forfeit his or her salvation. *"Those who are incorporated into Christ, ... Jesus Christ assists them ... and, if only they are ready for the conflict, and desire his help, and are not inactive, keeps them from falling. ... Whether they are capable ... of forsaking again the first beginnings of their life in Christ, ... that must be more particularly determined out of the Holy Scriptures." (Article V)*	**Perseverance dependent on God's will and work.** God works in the lives of Christians so that they persevere in faith to the end. *"God ... does not take the Holy Spirit from his own completely, even when they fall grievously. Neither does God let them fall down so far that they forfeit the grace of adoption and the state of justification. ... God preserves, continues, and completes this work by the hearing and reading of the gospel, by meditation on it, by its exhortations, threats, and promises, and also by the use of the sacraments." (Canons, V)*

Know More About...

There were many great strides in biblical teaching and theology taken in this era of Christian history. Yet conflict marked this era as well, and since most people could not yet imagine a church that wasn't partnered with the state, these conflicts sometimes led not only to division but also to death and destruction.

Arminianism and Calvinism

In any extended discussion of theology, the topic of Calvinism will eventually come up. Many people only know the supposed five points of Calvinism that are sometimes summed up in the acrostic TULIP: total depravity, unconditional election, limited atonement, irresistible grace, perseverance of the saints. But this acrostic isn't particularly accurate, and it didn't come from John Calvin or even from the 1618 Synod of Dort. In fact, TULIP was developed in the twentieth century, nearly four hundred years after the Synod of Dort.

Jacob Arminius (1560–1609)

Take a look at the chart in this chapter for a more accurate summary of seventeenth-century Arminian and Calvinist perspectives on salvation and predestination. Do you hold to a particular view—Calvinism or Arminianism? Why or why not?

_____

_____

_____

_____

_____

_____

Recognize that, for hundreds of years, faithful Christians have understood Scripture differently when it comes to the issue of predestination. Yet, in many instances, these Christians have been willing and able to work together in peace. Do you think that this is an issue that should divide congregations or denominations? Why or why not?

_____

_____

_____

_____

_____

Clashes between Protestants and Roman Catholics

In 1572, the Roman Catholic king of France ordered the assassinations of leading French Protestants in Paris. A few—but very few—magistrates refused to carry out the king's orders, declaring that they were neither executioners nor murderers. Most magistrates went along with the king's command. Parisian soldiers and mobs slaughtered about 3,000 Protestants in a single day, in what became known as the St. Bartholomew's Day Massacre. The violence then spread to other parts of France, leaving tens of thousands dead. The massacre led to a civil war and mistrust and strife between Catholics and Protestants for generations to come.

Refusing to go along with something that's wrong is not easy—especially when it feels like everyone is pressuring you be involved. Can you think of a time when you stood silent instead of standing up for what is right? What did you learn from that situation?

_____

_____

_____

_____

_____

Words from the Ones Who Were There

The Puritans

The Puritans wrote to King James I saying, "The church ought not to be governed by … any human invention, but by the laws and rules which Christ hath appointed in his Testament."

The Puritans passionately desired to remove anything from their churches that failed to fit what was allowed or implied in the New Testament. In what ways does the New Testament govern your church's worship? How about evangelism and ministry?

_____

_____

_____

_____

_____

Bartolome de las Casas

Many Europeans in the post-Reformation era argued that Native Americans and Africans could be enslaved because they were not human beings. Bartolome de las Casas, bishop of Chiapas, not only disagreed but he also risked his position by refusing Communion to anyone who abused Native Americans. "I have declared and demonstrated openly ... that all people of these our Indies are human, so far as is possible by the natural and human way and without the light of faith, [that they] had their republics, places, towns, and cities most abundant and well provided for, and did not lack anything to live politically and socially, and attain and enjoy civil happiness" (Apologética historia summaria de las gentes destas Indias).

Today, people are still enslaved and abused. Go to www.worldvision.org and search for information about Child Trafficking and Labor. Every human being is created in God's image; therefore, no human being should be reduced to a slave that is used and exploited by another human being. What will you do to speak out against enslavement and human trafficking today?

_____

_____

_____

_____

_____

Family Time

Get Together: Talk together about the following questions: What causes arguments or conflicts between people in our family? What might cause arguments or conflicts in churches?

Read Together: John 17:20–23 and Matthew 18:15–20

Learn Together: God desires unity and peace among his people. Jesus prayed these words in the Gospel of John only hours before his death.

Consider the pattern that Jesus provided in the passage from Matthew for maintaining unity and peace among his people. The patterns described by Jesus are possible only because Christians do not have to base their identity on whether they win a conflict. Jesus has already won the ultimate conflict! As a result, Christians don't have to focus on being proven right; they can speak the truth to one another with love and even confront one another. Talk about how you can apply this pattern in your church and in your home.

Pray Together: "Heavenly Father, we see how some have claimed the name of your Son, and yet they committed tremendous evils. We know that it is only by your grace that we do not follow in their footsteps. Work in us by your Spirit. Bring unity that is centered in the gospel in our family and in our church. In the name of Jesus Christ our Lord, Amen."

SESSION 10

Revolutions in the New World

AD *1600–1800*

Revolutionary ideas in the New World changed the way people saw the world. A small band of Pilgrims on the Mayflower, Puritans in Massachusetts, and one exiled man named Roger Williams forged different paths toward religious liberty. Meanwhile, the scientific revolution caused people to wonder, what if God merely created this machine-like world and then left us alone?

At a time when society was viewing God as increasingly distant, the Great Awakening would prove otherwise. A few unlikely men—a cross-eyed preacher named George Whitefield, a struggling missionary named John Wesley, and an unpopular gangly pastor named Jonathan Edwards—were all used by God to bring tidal waves of revival to the American colonies and beyond.

Session 10 Outline

1. Revolution in Religious Liberty

    a. "Saints" and "strangers" on the Mayflower landed in Plymouth (1620).

    b. Roger Williams founded Providence Colony on the idea of religious freedom (1636).

2. Revolution in Human Reason

    a. Isaac Newton described the universe as a machine.

    b. Deism and Enlightenment contributed to a rising focus on science and human reason as the primary means for making sense of life.

3. Revival and the Great Awakening

    a.   Moravian Pietists held a 100-year prayer meeting on the estate of Nikolaus von Zinzendorf in Germany.

    b.   John and Charles Wesley founded Methodism in England.

    c.   Jonathan Edwards led revival in American colonies.

    d.   George Whitefield preached to huge crowds in England and American colonies.

4. The American Revolution

Key Terms

Deism – Belief that God created the world but that he no longer acts directly or supernaturally in his world. Instead, he endowed the created order with natural laws that, if followed, lead to blessings.

Enlightenment – (also called the Age of Reason) Seventeenth- and eighteenth-century social and philosophical movement that emphasized reason as the primary source of authority, displacing divine revelation.

Methodist – Beginning as a Pietist movement, Methodism was established by John and Charles Wesley during the Great Awakening. Called "Methodist" because of their methodological approach to routines of prayer, fasting, Bible reading and other practices. Methodists hold to Arminian, not Calvinist views. Today, Methodists number 20–40 million worldwide.

Moravian Pietists – Also known as *Unitas Fratrum* or "Unity of the Brethren," they trace their roots back to Jan Hus in the fourteenth century. When they fled Moravia in 1722 they established the Herrnhut religious community in Saxony on the estate of Nikolaus von Zinzendorf.

Pietism – Seventeenth- and eighteenth-century Protestant movement that emphasized a life of personal discipline and devotion. The publication of Pious Desires by Lutheran pastor Philipp Jakob Spener marked an important beginning point for Pietism. Spener deeply influenced Nikolaus von Zinzendorf, who in turn influenced the Moravian Brothers and the Methodist movement.

Providence Colony – Colony in Rhode Island founded by Roger Williams in 1636 who defected from the Puritan-led Massachusetts Bay Colony. Williams established Providence with the intent of providing religious freedom.

Puritans – Protestants in sixteenth- and seventeenth-century England who wanted to purify the Church of England by reviving New Testament patterns of worship. Some Puritans from England sailed to America and settled the Massachusetts Bay Colony around the year 1630.

Revival (Great Awakening) – Revival is an unusual work of God by which God applies the gospel to his people in an unusually powerful way, resulting in salvation of sinners and renewed obedience among saints. The human means through which God works to bring revival are faithful proclamation of the gospel (Rom. 10:15–17) and fervent prayer among God's people (James 5:16). The Great Awakening in the mid-1700s in Europe and the American colonies is an example of revival.

Separatists – English Protestants who separated from the Church of England and formed independent congregations. The pilgrims on the Mayflower who settled Plymouth Colony in Massachusetts were Separatists.

Know More About...

In times when culture and society seem to be moving forward, it's easy to forget about God and even to live under the delusion that we are moving forward in our own power. That's partly why, seven times in the book of Deuteronomy, Moses warned the Israelites not to forget the God who had brought them out of Egypt (for example, Deut. 6:12).

Society and culture seemed to be moving forward in so many ways during the seventeenth and eighteenth centuries, and many people left behind the idea of a personal, all-powerful God. And yet, God raised up people who prayed for over a century, who protected the persecuted, and who proclaimed the gospel even when no one seemed to be listening.

The Enlightenment and Deism

The Enlightenment was a period in the seventeenth and eighteenth centuries that was marked by an emphasis on reason, science, progress, personal happiness, scientific inquiry, and endowed rights for all mankind. Isaac Newton and others had demonstrated how math and science could explain many of the universe's mysteries. As a result, the universe began to seem to many like a self-maintaining machine in which God was not necessary.

Instead of glorifying the Creator for his ongoing providence and recognizing their need for redemption through Jesus, many people turned to the false religion of Deism. Deists believed that God created the world, but that he no longer acted directly or supernaturally in the world. From a Deist perspective, humanity does not need salvation through faith in Jesus; people need only to follow the laws of nature and to imitate the ethics of Jesus.

Give yourself a few minutes to list as many similarities and differences as you can between people's views of God during the Enlightenment and people's views of God today.

Similarities between the Enlightenment and today	Differences between the Enlightenment and today

The Hundred-Year Nonstop Prayer Meeting

It started in 1727 (and yes, you read the heading correctly): twenty-four hours every day, seven days per week, for one hundred years! The participants were a group of Moravians meeting in a place called Herrnhut that was owned by a wealthy German nobleman, Count Nikolaus von Zinzendorf. Although relatively small in number, these Moravians eventually changed the world. The greatest significance of this movement was its impact on John Wesley and, through him, on the entire Methodist tradition.

How did this prayer meeting begin? Well, in some sense, it began in the late 1600s because of a movement known as Pietism. A man named Jacob Spener had written a booklet entitled Pious Desires. The book urged Christians to pursue a personal relationship with Christ through intense meditation on the Scriptures; this emphasis led to the rise of Pietism. The Pietists had a profound impact on Nikolaus von Zinzendorf.

In the early eighteenth century, several Catholic princes were persecuting the Moravian Brethren, a small group of Bohemian Protestants, and they became refugees. One rainy evening in 1722 a Moravian knocked on Zinzendorf's front

Nikolaus Zinzendorf (1700–1760)

door. He asked if Nikolaus Zinzendorf might shelter the flourishing Moravian movement. Nikolaus agreed. He helped the Moravians found a Christian community on his lands. They called their community "the Lord's watch" (or "Herrnhut"). By 1725, nearly one hundred Moravians had made Herrnhut their home.

If a group of refugees from the eighteenth century could start a century-long prayer meeting in a small corner of the world, what could you begin in your own community? Could you lead your family or your church in twenty-four hours of prayer? Perhaps twenty-four hours a day for a week?

In the space below, make specific plans for partnering with others in your church to take turns and to pray continuously for an extended period of time:

_____

_____

_____

_____

_____

_____

Words from the Ones Who Were There

Roger Williams

Roger Williams, who founded Providence Colony in Rhode Island, said this about the use of the power of the state in religious matters:

"A civil sword (as woeful experience in all ages has proved) is so far from bringing or helping forward an opposite in religion to repentance that magistrates sin grievously against the work of God and blood of souls by such proceedings.... To batter down idolatry, false worship, heresy, schism, blindness, hardness, out of the soul and spirit, it is vain, improper, and unsuitable to bring those weapons which are used by persecutors, stocks, whips, prisons, swords, gibbets, stakes, etc. ... but against these spiritual strongholds in the souls of men, spiritual artillery and weapons are proper."

A century later, this same sentiment was echoed in the U.S. Constitution: "Congress shall make no law respecting an establishment of religion, or prohibiting the free exercise thereof" (Bill of Rights, Amendment I).

Roger Williams believed that no civil state should attempt to enforce allegiance to a particular religious faith. Do you agree with Roger Williams? Why or why not?

_____

_____

_____

John Wesley

Throughout his life, John Wesley, the founded of the Methodist movement, kept a personal journal. The following sentences are from Wednesday, May 24, 1738.

John Wesley (1703–1791)

"In the evening I went very unwillingly to a society in Aldersgate Street, where one was reading Luther's preface to the Epistle to the Romans. About a quarter before nine, while he was describing the change which God works in the heart through faith in Christ, I felt my heart strangely warmed. I felt I did trust in Christ, Christ alone, for salvation; and an assurance was given me, that He had taken away my sins, even mine, and saved me from the law of sin and death."

Have you at any point in your life had a similar experience as John Wesley? In the space below, describe what that was like.

_____

_____

_____

Charles Wesley

Charles Wesley was more than just the brother of John Wesley. He is credited with writing more than 7,000 hymns, many of which Christians still sing today, such as "Christ the Lord is Risen Today," "Hark! The Herald Angels Sing," and "O for a Thousand Tongues to Sing."

He wrote in his hymn "And Can It Be that I Should Gain":

> "And can it be that I should gain / An interest in the Savior's blood! / Died he for me, who caused his pain! / For me? who him to death pursued? / Amazing love! How can it be / That thou, my God, shouldst die for me? / Amazing love! How can it be / That thou, my God, shouldst die for me?"

Three hundred years from now, what will people remember about you? I imagine Charles Wesley didn't realize the lasting impact that his words would have; he was simply using the gifts that God had given him to reach his own generation with the gospel. What are you doing that God might use to impact your world with the gospel?

_____

_____

_____

Jonathan Edwards

Jonathan Edwards, an American pastor and theologian, described the beginnings of the Great Awakening in this way:

"In the spring and summer following, [in the year] 1735, the town seemed to be full of the presence of God: it never was so full of love, nor of joy, and yet so full of distress, as it was then. There were remarkable tokens of God's presence in almost every house. It was a time of joy in families on account of salvation being brought to them; parents rejoicing over their children as newborn, and husbands over their wives, and wives over their husbands. The doings of God were then seen in his sanctuary, God's day was a delight, and his tabernacles were amiable. Our public assemblies were then beautiful: the congregation was alive in God's service, every one earnestly intent on the public worship, every hearer eager to drink in the words of the minister as they came from his mouth."

Jonathan Edwards (1703–1758)

What, from this description, are the characteristics of authentic revival? List as many characteristics of revival as you can find in the description. Then pray specifically that God will bring about these characteristics of revival in the lives of people in your church and community.

_____

_____

_____

_____

Family Time

Get Together: Have you ever failed to keep a commitment? You made clear resolutions. You had great intentions. Yet somehow you got off track. Jonathan Edwards made a resolution, and—even though he certainly didn't keep his resolution perfectly—his resolution did guide him toward deeper faithfulness to Jesus Christ.

Think back to New Year's Day this year. Discuss as a family any New Year's resolutions that you made. Talk about whether you kept them.

Read Together: Read Psalm 101 aloud together, perhaps having the males in your family read the odd-numbered verses and the females read the even-numbered verses. This psalm of David is filled with resolutions. "I will..." and other similar clauses appear over and over throughout the song.

Learn Together: At the age of eighteen, Jonathan Edwards wrote the following resolution in his journal: "Resolved: That all men should live to the glory of God. Resolved, secondly: That whether or not anyone else does, I will."

He became one of the key leaders in the Great Awakening, a powerful work of God about three hundred years ago in which thousands of sinners became believers and believers renewed their faithfulness to Jesus. The Great Awakening was not one single revival but a series of spontaneous awakenings happening at the same time and led by godly pastors in rural and village areas.

Work together to develop a resolution for your family. Print your resolution. If you have children, have them decorate the printed resolution. Give them the freedom to decorate it in their own way. Then, frame the decorated resolution; hang it in a prominent place in your house.

Pray Together: Pray phrase-by-phrase through Psalm 101. End your prayer by recognizing that only Jesus has perfectly followed these resolutions; he kept the law that none of us could keep so that all who believe will experience the eternal life that none of us deserves.

SESSION 11
Ageless Faith
in an Age of Reason
AD *1800–1900*

The Enlightenment cast aside faith and religion in favor of science and reason. Faith became a private thing—whatever works for you. The question that faced Christians in this era—and still faces believers today—was, if faith is just a personal matter, how do we show that the gospel of Jesus is needed by all people?

Christians responded to this emerging secular worldview in a variety of ways: A burgeoning missions movement was led by individuals such as William Carey, revivalists like Charles Spurgeon and Dwight Moody crisscrossed Europe and North America preaching a simple gospel message, liberal theologians tried to accommodate Christianity to the modern world, and the Catholic Church doubled-down on church authority.

Session 11 Outline

1. The Enlightenment ("Age of Reason")

    a. Scientific facts and human reason

2. Challenges to established authorities

    a. French Revolution cast aside the Catholic Church (1793).

    b. William Carey challenged Particular Baptists and began modern missions (1792).

    c. Church influence declined while a secular worldview emerged.

3. Five responses to the modern world

    a. Romanticism: Friedrich Schleiermacher tried to preserve Christianity with theological liberalism.

b. Reform: Sunday School (Robert Raikes), Temperance, Abolitionists

c. Revivalism

    i. Revival in Cane Ridge, Kentucky.

    ii. Barton Stone tried to end denominations.

    iii. Charles Finney's "philosophical" approach to revival.

    iv. Dwight L. Moody led evangelistic crusades.

    v. Charles Spurgeon preached the gospel in simple ways.

d. Resistance: First Vatican Council declared infallibility of the pope (1869).

e. Rejecting what we must, redeeming what we can: Niagara Bible Conference of 1895 agreed on five fundamentals.

Key Terms

Abolitionism – Movement in the 1700s and 1800s to abolish the trade in African slaves and eventually slavery itself.

Empiricism – Worldview that sees knowledge gained through scientific observation and the physical senses as primary, discounting knowledge gained through other sources and dismissing completely any knowledge that depends on divine revelation.

Enlightenment – (also called the Age of Reason) Seventeenth- and eighteenth-century social and philosophical movement that emphasized reason as the primary source of authority, displacing divine revelation.

First Vatican Council (1869-1870) – Over 700 Catholic bishops convened in Vatican City to deal with issues arising from modernism. The council confirmed the infallibility of the pope as church doctrine.

Fundamentals – Beliefs that had been denied in theologically liberal groups but which were emphasized strongly at certain Bible conferences throughout the late nineteenth and early twentieth centuries. Five of these fundamental beliefs were (1) inerrancy of Scripture, (2) deity of Jesus, (3) virgin conception of Jesus, (4) death of Jesus in place of sinners, and (5) bodily resurrection.

Industrial Revolution – Advancements in technology and transportation in the late 1700s and 1800s that shifted society from farm-based and home-based to an urban, factory-based society. Many people moved to cities to find work in factories.

Inerrancy – Belief that the inspired human authors of the Scriptures never affirmed anything contrary to fact when writing the texts that became part of the biblical canon; as a result, Christians can be confident that the Bible never errs.

Revival – A work of God by which the gospel is applied to people's lives in unusually powerful ways, resulting in salvation of sinners and renewed obedience among saints. The human means by which God brings revival are faithful proclamation of the gospel (Rom. 10:15–17) and fervent prayer among God's people (Acts 1:14; 2:42; see also Isaiah 63:15–64:12).

Revivalism – Religious movement beginning in the late eighteenth century that emphasized the use of human measures to bring about salvation and spiritual renewal. Revivalism was rooted in Nathaniel W. Taylor's New Haven theology and popularized by Charles Grandison Finney.

Romanticism – Eighteenth- and nineteenth-century reaction against Enlightenment rationalism and the Industrial Revolution; emphasized experience and emotion above reason and efficiency.

Temperance Movement – Social reform movement in the nineteenth and early twentieth centuries that promoted moderation or abstention in alcohol consumption.

Theological Liberalism – Theological movement that downplayed the authority of Scripture; theological liberals focused on the imitation of Christ's ethics and on living with a deep awareness of a divine presence in all of life. Friedrich Schleiermacher is sometimes called "the father of Protestant theological liberalism."

Five Fundamentals from the Niagara Bible Conference

Fundamental Belief	Explanation
Verbal inerrancy of Scripture	God inspired the very words of Scripture; these words, taken together, tell the truth and never err.
Deity of Christ	Jesus was and is fully God.
Virgin conception of Christ	Jesus was conceived through the power of the Holy Spirit and born of the Virgin Mary.
Vicarious expiation	On the cross, Jesus endured God's wrath against sin in place of every person who would trust in him. Also known as "substitutionary atonement."
Bodily resurrection of Jesus on the third day and of all humanity at the return of Christ	Jesus rose bodily from the grave on the third day; he will return to earth and raise to life the bodies of all humanity, both those made righteous through faith in him and those who will stand condemned.

The Two-Storied House

In the eighteenth and nineteenth centuries, people began to think in terms of a separation between the public sphere of scientific facts and reason, and the private or personal sphere of faith and values. In the minds of many people, Christian faith became relegated to private sphere and began to be seen as irrelevant to public discourse.

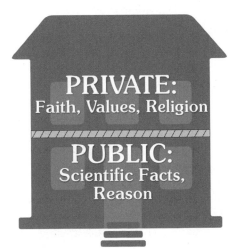

PRIVATE:
Faith, Values, Religion

PUBLIC:
Scientific Facts,
Reason

(Model based on Nancy Pearcey's description of the two-tiered view of truth in her book Total Truth.)

Know More About...

The world was changing! The Reformation had led to denominations. Global exploration had resulted in awareness of other cultures. The Enlightenment and empiricism resulted in skepticism about God's revelation of himself in Scripture. In the nineteenth century, those factors formed the background for the modern missions movement, revivalism, theological liberalism, and social reform.

Many of the movements and ideas in these centuries still shape our world in the twenty-first century. As you study this era in Christian history, consider carefully how understanding this time period can help you respond more wisely to the challenges that the church faces today.

Global Missions

William Carey once declared, "Expect great things from God! Attempt great things for God!" His life story was far from glamorous. Carey saw clearly that Calvinism can and should go hand-in-hand with a passion for global evangelism, yet many of Carey's fellow pastors disagreed with him. He was a struggling cobbler, a failed educator, a pastor with subpar preaching skills—not a track record that most would be proud of. Still, William Carey remained faithful. Even in the face of terrible tragedies—the deaths of two children, a depressed and deranged spouse, a fellow missionary who stole his funds, a fire that destroyed the fruits of his linguistic labors in India—Carey persevered. And what was the result? Within a century after Carey's death, the number of Christians living outside Europe and the Americas had increased at least one thousand percent!

Have you ever felt like God is asking you to do more than what you can do on your own? Perhaps he is! But that's precisely the point: God wants to do more through you than you could ever do in your own power, and he will equip you as you serve him. Read Ephesians 2:10.

William Carey (1761–1834)

How should these words from Paul encourage you to expect great things from God and to attempt great things for God?

_____

_____

_____

_____

Theological Liberalism

Friedrich Schleiermacher took the Pietist impulse in a different, more dangerous direction. Schleiermacher, sometimes called the "father of theological liberalism," tried to make Christianity relevant in the modern world by de-emphasizing doctrine and elevating a deep inner awareness of God. Christianity, in his view, did not require belief in certain facts about Jesus—such as the virgin birth, his death and resurrection, his deity, and so on. Instead, the essence of Christianity was a deep inner awareness that everyone has, and Jesus was the supreme example of such an experience.

Friedrich Schleiermacher (1768–1834)

Read Acts 17:22–34 where Paul addresses a pagan and skeptical crowd in Athens. Imagine if Paul met Schleiermacher. What might Paul say about Schleiermacher's view of Jesus and Scripture?

Words from the Ones Who Were There

Charles Dickens

British novelist Charles Dickens wrote these words regarding the late eighteenth century, the era of the French Revolution and the early Industrial Revolution: "It was the best of times, it was the worst of times."

As you survey this segment of history, consider the ways that Charles Dickens' famous words might apply. How was this era "the best of times"? What about it was "the worst of times"?

_____

_____

_____

_____

_____

Dwight L. Moody

"Well, by the Holy Spirit in me I'll be that man!" Moody uttered those words after hearing a fellow evangelist declare, "The world has yet to see what God can do with and for and through a man who is fully and wholly consecrated to him." Moody had only a fifth-grade education. Yet God used his preaching to bring millions of men and women to faith in Jesus Christ. Today, Moody's legacy continues not only through his sermons but also through educational institutions and Christian publishers.

Dwight L. Moody (1837–1899)

If you are a Christian, every part of your life already belongs to God (1 Cor. 6:19–20). Yet sometimes we live as if certain parts of our lives belong to us. That's why the apostle Paul called Christians to consecrate themselves wholly to God as "a living sacrifice." Take a few minutes to meditate on Paul's words in Romans 12:1–2. Perhaps read the verses two or three times.

Are there aspects of your life that you are treating as your own? List those areas in the space below. Specifically seek God's strength to respond to his grace by "fully and wholly" consecrating those aspects of your life to him.

_____

_____

_____

_____

_____

The Roman Catholic Church

In 1869, the First Vatican Council of the Roman Catholic Church declared that "the Roman pontiff [pope], when he speaks ... in discharge of the office of pastor and doctor of all Christians, ... [defining] a doctrine regarding faith or morals to be held by the universal Church, by the Divine assistance promised to him in Blessed Peter, he is possessed of that infallibility with which the Divine Redeemer willed that his Church should be endowed in defining doctrine regarding faith or morals, and that therefore such definitions of the Roman pontiff are of themselves, and not from the consent of the Church, irreformable. So then, should anyone, which God forbid, have the temerity to reject this definition of ours: let him be anathema."

In other words, the First Vatican Council stated that the pope is infallible whenever he "defines a doctrine." Anyone who rejects this is declared "anathema," that is, set aside for destruction. The infallibility of the pope was upheld and clarified nearly a century later in 1965 at the Second Vatican Council, and continues to be a Roman Catholic teaching today.

What specific difficulties does this declaration present when it comes to dialogue between the Roman Catholic Church and Eastern Orthodox or Protestant churches?

_____

_____

_____

_____

Family Time

Get Together: Has there ever been a time when you lost focus? Maybe it was while driving a car or while playing a sport. Perhaps it was in a classroom or while doing your homework. Talk as a family about these experiences as well as the consequences of losing focus on something that matters. Then, discuss what should be the ultimate focus in life: Jesus. He must be the central focus because he is the only one to whom all glory belongs and through whom sinners can be made right with God. Any spiritual power that we may have is only because of the Holy Spirit that Jesus has placed in his people (John 14:15–17, 25–27). Anything that we do apart from this power is meaningless.

Read Together: Read John 15:4–5

Learn Together: Charles Haddon Spurgeon was a pastor in England during the 1800s. He was committed to helping the poor and caring for orphans. But this love for the poor flowed out of his commitment to the gospel of Jesus Christ. Throughout Spurgeon's ministry, the focus of his ministry remained on Jesus. Spurgeon clearly recognized that he could do nothing meaningful in his own power; his power came through the Spirit that Jesus placed in his people beginning on the day of Pentecost. In a sermon entitled "The Outpouring of the Holy Spirit," Spurgeon declared, "Let the preacher always confess before he preaches that he relies upon the Holy Spirit. Let him burn his manuscript and depend upon the Holy Spirit. If the Spirit does not come to help him, let him be still and let the people go home and pray that the Spirit will help him next Sunday." Learn more about Charles Haddon Spurgeon at www.spurgeon.org.

Pray Together: Read John 14:27. Talk about how the peace of Jesus is possible for Christians because we abide in Jesus, resting in him and trusting that nothing can come into our lives that he has not allowed. Consider how the peace of Jesus might look like in your lives. Pray specifically for this peace in your family and in your church.

SESSION 12
A Global Gospel
AD *1900–Present*

In the early twentieth century, many people were optimistic that all Christian groups—from Catholics to Protestants and fundamentalists to liberals—could be brought together to reach the world with the gospel. But what is the gospel? Every generation must answer that question. Evangelists like Billy Graham, theologians like Karl Barth, and trailblazers like Dietrich Bonhoeffer sought to articulate the gospel message for their generation.

In the twenty-first century, we too must continue that same mission of communicating the gospel, and stand firmly on the assurance that whatever the future holds, God will always be faithful to preserve his church.

Session 12 Outline

1. Twentieth-Century Optimism

    a. Holiness Movement; Charles Fox Parham encouraged his students
        to seek the gift of speaking in tongues (1901).

    b. Azusa Street Revival (1906); William Seymour founded Pentecostalism.

    c. World Missionary Conference was held to bring denominations
        together (1910).

2. Fundamentalism and Liberalism

    a. Harry Emerson Fosdick preached "Shall the Fundamentalists
        Win?" (1922).

    b. J. Gresham Machen defined liberalism as a different religion from
        Christianity (1923).

    c. "Neo-orthodox" theology was promoted through Karl Barth's
        commentary on Romans (1919).

d. Dietrich Bonhoeffer urged German churches to resist Nazism.

3. The Ecumenical Movement

a. World Council of Churches brought together neo-orthodox and liberals (1948).

b. National Association of Evangelicals helped to distinguish evangelicals from fundamentalists (1942).

c. Billy Graham launched large-scale evangelistic meetings (1949).

d. Carl F. H. Henry wrote *The Uneasy Conscience of Modern Fundamentalism* (1947).

e. Lausanne Covenant helped define evangelicalism (1974)

f. Second Vatican Council removed the sentences of excommunication between Catholic Church and Eastern Orthodox (1962–1965).

g. Manhattan Declaration expressed common ground between churches on social issues (2009).

Key Terms

Azusa Street Revival (1906)

– Often considered the beginning of modern Pentecostalism, this revival was led by African-American pastor William Seymour and located at the Apostolic Faith Mission on Azusa Street in Los Angeles. It emphasized the filling of the Holy Spirit, speaking in tongues, holiness, and faith healing.

Apostolic Faith Gospel Mission in Los Angeles, California

Barmen Declaration (1934)

– Statement that came from a meeting of German Protestant leaders in Barmen, Germany, held to oppose the so-called "German Christians" who were reinterpreting Christianity to conform to Nazi ideology. The Declaration's principal author was Karl Barth.

Ecumenical Movement – Movement that aimed to bring together Catholics, Protestants, Orthodox and other churches. The World Missionary Conference of 1910 and the World Council of Churches founded in 1948 were expressions of the ecumenical movement.

Evangelical (Neo-evangelical) – Expression of Christianity that seeks to establish and to maintain faithfulness to the biblical and confessional foundations of Christianity by emphasizing (1) the accuracy and authority of Scripture, (2) the exclusivity of salvation through personal faith in Jesus Christ, (3) the centrality of the sacrifice of Jesus Christ on the cross, (4) the need for global evangelism and cultural engagement, and (5) unity among like-minded Christians. In the nineteenth century and earlier, "evangelical" had been a synonym for "Protestant." In the twentieth century, the term "neo-evangelical" or "new evangelical" emerged to describe Christians who (unlike modernists) recognized Scripture as their authority and who (unlike fundamentalists) wanted to engage the culture instead of withdrawing from the culture. Eventually, "neo-evangelical" became simply "evangelical."

Fundamentalist – Twentieth-century fundamentalists resisted modernism by fighting verbally against any perceived threats to non-negotiable (or "fundamental") beliefs; many withdrew from meaningful engagement with the culture and lengthened their lists of non-negotiable beliefs to include for example, exclusive use of the King James Version and a pre-tribulational premillennial view of the end times. By the mid-twentieth century, "fundamentalists" typically referred to conservative Christians who focused on precise personal standards and on separation from every hint of liberalism.

Holiness Movement – Nineteenth-century movement that grew out of the Methodist church and focused on Christian sanctification. Holiness followers adhered to strict moral guidelines and abstained from worldly amusements. In the twentieth century some Holiness leaders, such as Charles Fox Parham, embraced speaking in tongues and faith healing.

Lausanne Covenant (1974) – Statement developed in Lausanne, Switzerland, at a convention—chaired by Billy Graham—of over 2,700 Christian leaders worldwide. This covenant became influential in defining evangelicalism.

Manhattan Declaration (2009) – Statement that recognized commonalities among evangelicals, conservative Protestants, Roman Catholics, and Orthodox on three specific moral issues: (1) profound, inherent, and equal dignity of every human being, (2) marriage as a conjugal union of man and woman, and (3) religious liberty.

Neo-orthodoxy –Theological movement, initiated by Swiss pastor Karl Barth, that reacted against theological liberalism by emphasizing God's sovereign self-revelation as the authority for Christian faith and practice. Unlike fundamentalists and evangelicals, Barth did not view Scripture as the inerrant written revelation of God. Instead, Scripture is a witness to Jesus, who is the one Word of God. Many neo-orthodox theologians eventually embraced patterns of thinking that were similar to theological modernism.

Pentecostalism – Expression of Christianity that emphasizes baptism by the Holy Spirit and speaking in tongues. Their name comes from the events described in Acts 2 when the Holy Spirit filled the disciples on the Day of Pentecost. Though distinct from the Holiness Movement, many early Pentecostals came from Holiness churches.

Second Vatican Council (1962) – Allowed translation of liturgies into native languages, recognized that non-Catholics "are not deprived of significance … in the mystery of salvation," and declared that "no one is to be forced [by ones' government] to act in a manner contrary to one's beliefs," but no key doctrine that separates Roman Catholics from Protestants, such as justification by faith or the extent of the pope's power, was changed.

Theological Liberalism (also, Theological Modernism) – Nineteenth-century movement that downplayed the authority of Scripture, focusing instead on imitation of Christ's ethics and on living with a deep awareness of a divine presence in all of life. Theological liberals altered Christian theology to fit the outlook of the modern world by separating Christian theology from traditional doctrines and biblical texts. In the twentieth century, theological liberalism developed into a movement that saw Christian principles as a foundation for accommodating the values of the culture. The twentieth-century American form of theological liberalism was known as theological modernism.

Know More About...

Twentieth-Century Optimism

Optimism marked the opening years of the twentieth century. In the minds of many people, it seemed as if all Christians—or, at least, all Protestants—might soon unite to spread the claims of Christianity around the globe. New discoveries would end suffering and disease. Education would bring social and economic equality.

By the midpoint of the twentieth century, two world wars and an economic depression had shattered this optimism. "Scientists ... were churning out the idea that science was going to transform the world. Science and education would make everything wonderfully different," evangelical theologian J.I. Packer recalled, reflecting on his years as a schoolboy in the first half of the twentieth century. "In the early months of the Second World War, the plausibility of that began to diminish rapidly."

During the first half of the twentieth century, Protestantism fragmented into fundamentalists, modernists, and evangelicals. Before the century was over, there would be even more fragments. At the same time, a degree of unity began to emerge among evangelicals who embraced the truthfulness of Scripture and who saw themselves not only as pilgrims to another world, but also as ambassadors and change agents in this world. This is the world in which you and I now live, in the first half of the twenty-first century.

Modernism and Fundamentalism

Harry Emerson Fosdick, a leading modernist, once declared, "These are the things we have stood for: tolerance, an inclusive Church, the right to think religion through in modern terms, the social applications of the principles of Jesus.... They call me a heretic. I am proud of it."

Fundamentalism arose to protect essential Christian beliefs against theological liberalism and modernism. According to Curtis Lee Laws, who first applied the term "fundamentalist," fundamentalists were Christians who were "ready to do battle royal for the fundamentals of the faith." Early twentieth-century fundamentalists resisted modernism by fighting verbally against any perceived threats to non-negotiable (or "fundamental") beliefs.

Over time, many fundamentalists separated from meaningful engagement with the culture and lengthened their lists of non-negotiable beliefs for which they were "ready to do battle." Eventually, some fundamentalists demanded adherence to such beliefs as the exclusive use of the King James Version, a certain view of the end times, creation in six twenty-four-hour days, and even particular standards for clothing and music. These fundamentalists called for complete separation from anyone who did not share their beliefs.

What was positive about the fundamentalist movement in the early twentieth century? And what was negative?

_____

_____

_____

_____

_____

_____

Pentecostalism

In 1900 an evangelist named Charles Fox Parham founded a Bible institute in Topeka, Kansas. Parham taught his students that "speaking with other tongues" should accompany "the second blessing"—an act of the Spirit that could result in "Christian perfection."

On January 1, 1901, one of Parham's students began to speak in a language that no one in the Bible institute recognized. Nearly all the students went as missionaries to other countries, believing they had received the capacity to speak in languages unknown to them.

Five years later, Parham's perspective had reached California. William Seymour, an African-American preacher, preached the Pentecostal message at the Apostolic Faith Gospel Mission on Azusa Street in Los Angeles.

William J. Seymour (1870–1922)

Many of Seymour's hearers also seemed to speak in languages unknown to them. Soon, hundreds were flocking to Azusa Street to experience "baptism with the Holy Ghost." Pentecostalism spread as people returned to their churches convinced that speaking in unknown tongues should accompany the second blessing. In 1914, several Pentecostal groups merged to form the Assemblies of God.

Even if you are not Pentecostal, consider what aspects of the Pentecostal movement were admirable and helpful. List some of these positive contributions below:

_____

_____

_____

_____

_____

Words from the Ones Who Were There

Twentieth-Century Christian Leaders

Every generation faces its own form of "the battle for the Bible"—the struggle to see Scripture as God's sufficient and authoritative testimony for his people in every time and every place. Reflect carefully on these words about the Bible from twentieth-century Christian leaders:

Dietrich Bonhoeffer (Letter to Ruediger Schleicher): "If it is I who determine where God is to be found, then I shall always find a God who corresponds to me in some way, who is obliging, who is connected with my own nature. But if God determines where he is to be found, then it will be in a place which is not immediately pleasing to my nature and which is not at all congenial to me. This place is the Cross of Christ. And whoever would find him must go to the foot of the Cross, as the Sermon on the Mount commands. This is not according to our nature at all, it is entirely contrary to it. But this is the message of the Bible, not only in the New but also in the Old Testament.... Since I have learnt to read the Bible in this way—and this has not been for so very long—it becomes every day more wonderful to me. I read it in the morning and the evening, and often during the day as well, and every day I consider a text which I have chosen for the whole week, and try to sink deeply into it, so as really to hear what it is saying. I know that without this I could not live properly."

Karl Barth (Barmen Declaration): "Jesus Christ, as he is attested for us in Holy Scriptures, is the one Word of God, which we hear and which we have to trust and obey in life and death."

Lausanne Covenant: "We affirm the divine inspiration, truthfulness and authority of both Old and New Testament Scriptures in their entirety as the only written word of God, without error in all that it affirms, and the only infallible rule of faith and practice."

Read the following passages. Write down one or two things that each passage tells us about what Scripture is and what it is for.

John 17:17 _____

_____

2 Timothy 3:14–17 _____

_____

2 Peter 1:16–21 _____

_____

2 Peter 3:15–17 _____

_____

Carl F. H. Henry

In his groundbreaking book The Uneasy Conscience of Modern Fundamentalism, Carl F. H. Henry pointed out how many conservative Christians had worked so hard to separate themselves from modernism that they had retreated from meaningful engagement with their culture: "Whereas once the redemptive gospel was a world-changing message, now it was narrowed to a world-resisting message.... For the first protracted period in its history, evangelical Christianity stands divorced from the great social reform movements.... While we are pilgrims here, we are ambassadors also."

How has the situation changed—or stayed the same—since Carl F. H. Henry wrote these words in 1947?

_____

_____

_____

_____

H. Richard Niebuhr

In 1937, theologian H. Richard Niebuhr summarized the liberal gospel as, "A God without wrath brought men without sin into a kingdom without judgment through the ministrations of a Christ without a Cross."

Read John 17:13–18 and 1 John 2:15–17. Summarize in your own words how Christians today should engage the culture and transform the culture without conforming the Christian faith to fit the culture.

_____

_____

_____

_____

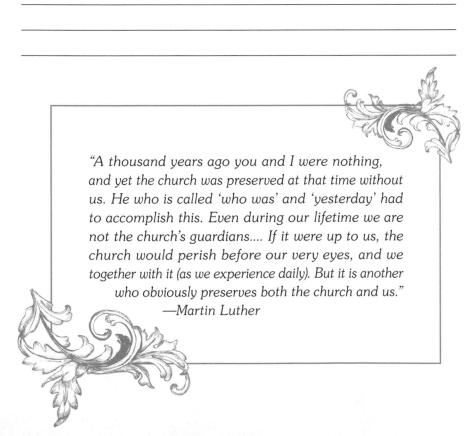

"A thousand years ago you and I were nothing, and yet the church was preserved at that time without us. He who is called 'who was' and 'yesterday' had to accomplish this. Even during our lifetime we are not the church's guardians.... If it were up to us, the church would perish before our very eyes, and we together with it (as we experience daily). But it is another who obviously preserves both the church and us."
—*Martin Luther*

Family Time

Get Together: Have each person bring an item to family time that they have saved money to purchase. Ask: Did you know how much this would cost when you began saving money to purchase it? Talk together about counting the cost.

Read Together. Read 2 Corinthian 11:24–27. These verses describe what it cost Paul to be faithful to the gospel of Jesus Christ. Discuss what it means to count the cost of responding faithfully to Jesus.

Learn Together. "When Christ calls a man, he bids him come and die." The man who wrote those words was a German Christian named Dietrich Bonhoeffer. When given the chance to remain safe in the United States, Bonhoeffer replied, "I shall have no right to participate in the reconstruction of Christian life in Germany after the war if I do not share the trials of this time with my people." On April 9, 1945, Bonhoeffer was executed for working to overthrow Adolf Hitler's regime.

Corrie ten Boom was a Christian in Holland who hid Jewish persons during the Holocaust. Her father and her sister Betsie died in Nazi concentration camps. Yet she declared, "There is no pit so deep that God's love is not deeper still.... God will give us the love to be able to forgive our enemies." Look together as a family at www.corrietenboom.com.

Talk together about persecuted Christians throughout the world today. (See www.persecution.org or www.opendoorsusa.org to learn more.) Allow each family member to share at least one way that following Jesus may become costly in his or her life.

Pray Together. "Father, how deeply we desire your name to be glorified in the languages of every people group! Make us willing to embrace the cost of proclaiming the gospel of Jesus Christ among all the nations. Move in these nations by your Spirit to bring true and lasting revival. Amen."

Other DVD-Based Studies
For Individuals or Group Use

Christianity, Cults & Religions
Know what you believe and why!

Christians need to know what they believe. This excellent six-session DVD small group study teaches what the Bible says about God, Jesus, salvation, and more. It compares it to the teachings of other religions and cults. Covers Mormonism, Jehovah's Witnesses, Buddhism, Hinduism, Islam and more. Sessions led by Paul Carden, Director of The Centers for Apologetics Research and former co-host of "Bible Answer Man" radio program.

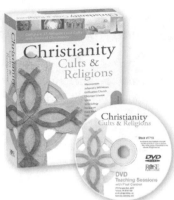

771X	Complete Kit	9781596364134
771DV	DVD	9781596364271
784X	Leaders Guide	9781596364288
785X	Participants Guide	9781596364295
404X	Christianity, Cults & Religions pamphlet	9789901981403

Four Views of the End Times
Cut through the confusion about the *Book of Revelation*

What does the Bible actually say about the end times that lead to the return of Jesus Christ? The differing ideas that divide believers into four major points-of-view are examined in this Four Views of the End Times DVD-based small group study. This new six-session study shows four different Revelation time lines and tackles Dispensational Premillennialism, Postmillennialism, Historic Premillennialism, and Amillennialism. For each view, the objective study includes simple definitions, explanation and discussion of supporting Scriptures, an overview of the view's popularity, and a focus on what we can gain from studying this perspective, and common questions and answers.

770X	Complete Kit	9781596364127
770DV	DVD	9781596364240
782X	Leader Guide: Four Views	9781596364257
783X	Participants Guide: Four Views	9781596364264
350X	Four Views of the End Times pamphlet	9781596360891

Feasts of the Bible
Connect the Hebrew roots of Christianity and the symbolism within each feast

Some Christians miss the importance of the biblical feasts, seeing them as merely "Jewish" holidays, but Scripture says these are the Feasts of the Lord God, established for all people for all time. Now you can connect the Hebrew roots of Christianity and the symbolism within each feast that points to Jesus Christ. The Feasts and Holidays of the Bible will also show you how to conduct your own Christian Passover Seder, where you will learn how all the Old Testament Passover activities point symbolically to Jesus.

101X	Complete Kit	9781596364646
101DV	DVD	9781596364653
102X	Leaders Guide	9781596364660
103X	Participants Guide	9781596364677
455X	Feasts of the Bible pamphlet	9781890947583
108X	Messiah in the Feasts of Israel book	9780970261977